Occupy Gooberville

For the 99% of you who actually think my answers are right

by Clay Thompson

AMERICAN
TRAVELER PRESS

Phoenix, Arizona

Occupy Gooberville

American Traveler Press
5738 North Central Avenue
Phoenix, Arizona 85012
www.claythompsonbooks.com
info@AmericanTravelerPress.com
(800) 521-9221

Cover design by ATG Productions, LLC., Christy Moeller-Masel — www.atgproductions.com
Interior design by The Printed Page, Lisa Liddy — www.theprintedpage.com

ISBN 978-0-935810-94-3

For Julia Wallace,
whose idea this was in the first place.

Contents

Foreword

If I had known that Clay had time to work on his third book I would have made him write another column each week. Oh wait, there are only seven days in a week and he's already got them all covered. I guess he's the master of time management, and I'm just the guy who wants to get as much blood out of the turnip as possible. I hope his loyal followers enjoy this collection.

Randy Lovely
Editor, *The Arizona Republic*

Acknowledgments

First of all, about the title. A friend suggested that the whole Occupy movement might be out of style within a few months of this book coming out so maybe I should have picked a more long-lasting title.

I suppose my friend might be right, but the fact of the matter is that "goober" is fun to say. Try it. Say "goober" out loud several times in a row.

"Goober, goober, goober, goober, goober, goober."

See? Don't you feel better already? I know I do.

Next, when I originally wrote the columns collected here I thought they were pretty darn good. Or at least pretty darn OK.

But when I went back to reread them and pick them out for this book they struck me as kind of lame. I hope you've already paid for this when you read that. I need the money.

I have several people to thank for mess.

First of all, my readers. Either because a failure of our education system or the general decline of Western civilization, many of you seem to enjoy the column. I appreciate that.

Next, my masters. I know I snark on them, but they let me get away with that and a lot of other stuff.

I especially need to thank my immediate editors, especially *The Republic's* copy editors who have saved me more than once from sounding like a complete idiot.

My New Years Resolutions of 2008

December 30, 2007

Have you made any New Year's resolutions? I have and for a change I'm going to keep them instead of forgetting about them in a couple of weeks.

For one thing, I resolve to eat more pie in 2008. And I am going to work on my laziness habit. It might take some doing, but I bet if I really buckle down I can be even lazier in the new year than I have been this year. Call me idealistic. Call me high-minded, but I can do it.

And I'm going to get started on it as soon as I take care of this lady's question.

As a woman of a certain age who has to cross her legs each time she sneezes (way too information, I know) it has come to my attention that sneezes can be overwhelmingly powerful forces of nature. Are sneezes rated in any way by the amount of force or energy they emit? Like a Richter scale for sneezes?It took me a minute to figure out the crossing-your-legs thing. You're right, lady—too much information.

Did you know that some Buddhist teachings hold that sneezing can give you a kind of low-level experience of near-death awareness and what they call "clear light?" I guess this is supposed to be a good thing.

Anyway, as far as I can tell no one has ever devised a scale for rating the force of sneezes.

However, I can tell you a good hearty sneeze can propel about 5,000 germy droplets up to 12 feet at around 100 mph.

You don't want to go around spreading contagion by sneezing on people, but it also is not a good idea to stifle a sneeze. That can send a powerful rush of air up your Eustachian tubes and might damage your ears.

And speaking of sneezing:

Why do cold symptoms seem to get worse at night?

They don't really. You're just more aware of them.

During the day your brain keeps itself busy analyzing stimuli, sending out messages and just running the show in general. But when you are asleep, your brain doesn't have as many things on its mind, so to speak, so it can pay more attention to the fact that you're sick.

&#@) MP3 player

January 17, 2008

I RECENTLY acquired an MP3 player. Or maybe it's mp3. I don't know. I'm not quite sure what it is, but I am working on it. In fact, I have spent the better part of the day working on it, and I am about to wedge it against the tires and back over it.

I have some friends with small children, and those children confidently told me they would fix it up for me.

I would rather eat dirt than have to admit to these two charming, bright children that I can't figure this thing out. I'd never hear the end of it.

So I'm cranky. Again. And today's question has not done much to improve my disposition.

How many United States presidents have been left-handed? Does that make a difference in their ability to be elected to a second term? Who was the most prestigious of the left-handed presidents? Are you people all on something lately that I am somehow missing out on by hanging around the house all the time in my bathrobe to the dogs? I really need to get out more.

Ah, well, if I did get paid the big bucks this is the sort of thing I'd get paid the big bucks for, I suppose.

Left-handed presidents: James A. Garfield, Herbert Hoover, Harry S. Truman, Gerald Ford, Ronald Reagan, George H.W. Bush and Bill Clinton.

As for the electability or prestige of left-handed presidents, I'll let you guys decide. You seem to have plenty of time on your hands to ponder such matters.

How did the Joshua tree get its name?

Mormon settlers crossing the desert thought the tree resembled the Biblical figure Joshua raising his arms to the sky to command the sun to stop because his army needed more daylight to finish killing whoever it was they were killing.

The tree has several other names, including desert orange. The story has it that land speculators studded trees' branches with oranges to fool buyers into thinking the desert were fertile land.

You'd have to be kind of dumb to fall for that one. I wonder if anyone ever did.

Learn to speak Phoenix-ese with ease

January 19, 2008

So I finally got that MP3 thing figured out. As a matter of fact, I now can MP3 with the best of them, even without the help of my friends' young children who supposedly can MP3 with one hand while doing their homework with the other and still talk on the phone.

Who needs 'em?

Of course I had to call their mother about 18 times to talk me through it, but that doesn't count. I didn't call their father because just between you and me I suspect he has his kids do that MP3 stuff for him. He seemed a little vague about the whole thing.

So now with my ears plugged up with a constant flow of music that I suspect nobody likes but me, let's get down to work.

Would you be so kind as to tell me if Jomax Road is pronounced as "Joemax" or "Yoemax" or "Hoemax"? And is Jokake Road pronounced "Joekake" or "Yoekake" or "Hoekake"? Since La Jolla is La "Hoya" and San Jacinto is San "Yahcinto" the pronunciations of these Phoenix-area streets have me baffled.

New to these parts, aren't you, stranger?

Jomax, as in Jomax Road, is pronounced "Joe-max." The story I have always heard is that the guy who first developed the area and laid out the road named it for his two daughters, who it seems were named Joanne or Josephine and Maxine, or some variations of those names.

And as for Jokake Road goes, according to Will Barnes' most excellent Arizona Place Names it started out as the name of a resort on the south slope of Camelback Mountain.

Its first buildings were made of adobe, and when a Hopi who worked on the construction was asked to suggest for a name for the place he suggested Jokake, pronounced "Jo-cocky," which in his language meant, "mud house."

You have to bear in mind that while places such as Tucson or many other towns south of Gila River and many California cities started out as mostly Hispanic communities, Phoenix started out as a mostly Anglo town. So the fine points of pronunciation—such as the "J" in Hispanic words—tended to get glossed over.

Why would you want to do this anyway?

February 11, 2008

Can you shred paper in a garbage disposal without gumming up the disposal? If my kitchen garbage disposal will eviscerate and incinerate all types of hard food, I wondered if it would shred paper. I thought I'd ask you before I try it. There is much here that I do not understand.

First of all, I assume you are exaggerating when you say your disposal will "incinerate" stuff you put in it. You do know that to incinerate something means to burn it up, don't you? I'm never quite sure about you people.

Next, why would you want to shred paper in your garbage disposal in the first place? I don't get it. What would the point of that be?

Why don't you either put in the recycle bin or in the garbage? Or in a compost heap or a worm bed?

Anyway, I suppose the occasional paper towel wouldn't hurt anything, but in general I think you should keep paper out of the disposal. And your hands, too.

One of the puzzle answers on a recent Wheel of Fortune was "bobby pins." My husband questioned the spelling, saying he thought it was "bobbie" not "bobby." Then we wondered why they are called bobby/bobbie pins in the first place.

First of all, it's "bobby' and not "bobbie." Your husband shouldn't be so uppity about doubting Wheel of Fortune. Who does he think he is?

Secondly, bobby pin goes back to the 1920s when the bobbed cut or bobbed hair came into fashion.

Where did the phrase "neck of the woods," meaning a neighborhood or locale, come from? It is an Americanism going back to colonial times when a "neck" meant a narrow strip of timber or pasture or whatever. It came to mean a small or remote settlement in the forest, and went on to be used to mean a district or area or stuff like that. It first appeared in print in the sense that we use it today in 1839.

The New Jersey towns of Penn Neck and Dutch Neck no doubt started out as small towns in the woods.

Sweaty legs

February 28, 2008

Why don't our legs sweat?

Who told you your legs don't sweat?

I just don't know where you people pick up these ideas. Do you hear them on one of those talk radio stations or one of those unattributed Internet pages? Sometimes I worry that you people get a lot of your information about your bodily functions on the schoolyard or from your morning coffee groups or in the gutter, so to speak.

It's good thing you have me around to explain these things to you, or at least it's a good thing on the days I actually might get something right.

In the course of all this, I read that horses don't have sweat glands in their legs, although I never found anything that backed that up. I wonder if that's true, and, if so, why. I'll have to look into that one some more. Maybe after my nap.

Anyway, the average person has about 2.6 million sweat glands, although I don't know who first counted them. And plenty of those glands are in your legs.

You come outfitted with two types of sweat glands. You have eccrine sweat glands, also known as merocrine glands. They're the ones that do a lot of the heavy lifting, sweat-wise.

And you have apocrine sweat glands, which are located in your armpits and naughty bits and when they produce sweat it mingles with bacteria on your skin to produce a kind of…umm…aroma.

Your eccrine or merocine sweat glands are all over the place, including your legs, and they're the ones in your palms and soles of your feet and your forehead that make you all damp when you get flop sweat.

However, in the order of things the eccrine sweat glands in your legs are among the last to kick in, unless they are in direct contact with the source of heat. But they crank out the sweat nonetheless.

Not to be indelicate, but haven't you ever had a heat rash on your inner thighs?

Part of the reason for that is that your legs are sweating. If that sweat can't escape your skin gets too warm and you get those itchy little red bumps.

Harass hawks or leave them alone?

March 11, 2008

We bought a home 12 years ago that has a rock waterfall and spa. Unfortunately the previous owner planted three palm trees behind the spa. The palms are now tall and Harris hawks sit in them and poop on the cover of the spa, on the waterfall, and surrounding area. Our grandchildren will be coming, and they love our spa. How can I keep the hawks away? I thought about scaring them with a pellet gun, but I understand they are an endangered species.

Hmm. I'm not too sure I can help you out.

First of all, Harris hawks are not considered to be especially endangered, but they are protected by the Migratory Bird Treaty Act. So you can't just go around shooting at them. Why is it that you people always want to shoot things that annoy you?

You could try having the palms trimmed back to the point that they didn't offer the hawks a secure roost, but I don't think the hawks need too much space to perch on, so that might or might not work.

And don't try to do the trimming yourself. At your age I don't want you wobbling around on a tall ladder and waving a saw around.

Do you have bird feeders or quail blocks in your yard? If so, that might be what's attracting the hawks—easy prey. Try removing the feeders for a week or so and see if the hawks leave.

Harris hawks do have predators, or at least predators that prey on their young. Ravens and coyotes and great horned owls. You could put up some of those fake owls, but I suspect the hawks would just peck them to pieces.

Or if you put your mind to it, you could find some recordings of ravens or coyotes or owls and broadcast them, although your neighbors might not be too crazy about this.

Or consider this: The hawks and their ancestors were there before you. Maybe you should just hose off your spa cover and the patio as needed and remember that when you live on the desert you live with hawks and other stuff. Show the hawks to your grandkids and teach them to appreciate such wonders.

Just don't shoot them, OK?

Reversing a Glendale driving story

March 26, 2008

I have heard that it is illegal for a car to back up in the City of Glendale. If this were true, wouldn't it be illegal to back out of your own driveway?

Well, I've heard that on certain days of the year my masters sprout tails and their eyes turn sort of red and they lope around their neighborhoods on all fours making strange sort of slathering noises.

That doesn't necessarily make it so.

I suppose if I happened to be a tireless, hard-working investigative kind of guy, I could have made a bunch of calls about this or done some hard-hitting interviews. But that probably would have involved putting on pants and wearing real shoes.

So instead I went to my old favorite, www.snopes.com, where they specialize in debunking stuff like this. It turned out they had a whole page to debunking stories about loony laws in Arizona.

This is what they had to say about driving in reverse in Glendale:

"Some people pose enough of a hazard when driving forwards, but neither the Glendale City Attorney's Office nor the Glendale Police Department knows of any law against driving cars in reverse."

You should check this site out. There is a bunch of stuff about whether it is illegal to wear suspenders in Nogales or to play cards on the street with a Native American in Globe or if it's illegal for women to wear pants in Tucson.

The full address is: www.snopes.com/legal/arizona.asp.

I am wondering where the "luke" in "lukewarm" comes from. There is no "lukecool."

Of course there isn't any "lukecool." That would be silly.

The "luke" part of lukewarm goes all the way back to the Old English word hleow, which meant "tepid."

Old English people spoke Old English from about the 600's to the 1300's, when, I guess they switched to Not-So-Old English, or something like that.

Six young ladies do not constitute a brothel

April 10, 2008

I'm a student at Arizona State University, and I'm looking into renting a house with five friends. However, I hear there is a law in Tempe that makes it illegal for six or more unrelated women to live together, on the grounds that it is a brothel. I can't figure out if this is true or not, and if it is, what the penalty is. Can you help me out?

Go ahead and move in with your pals. I don't know what social dynamics are involved in six young women living together, but apparently it is OK in the eye of the law.

There are a whole bunch of those half-baked "stupid laws" websites out there that claim there is such a six-women-brothel law in Maricopa County, but if there ever was it has long since been repealed. Even if there were such a law on the books, I'm sure our county law enforcement people have better things to do than try to enforce it, aren't you? I mean, there are all those people out there with cracked windshields and burned-out turn signals.

According to snopes.com—my favorite myth busters—the brothel-law thing is a fairly common story that gets passed around in college towns. Snopes could find no such law on anybody's books.

Look at it this way: If there were such a law there wouldn't be any sororities, would there?

So go ahead and move in with your friends. Just make sure you all agree ahead of time about stuff like money and chores.

Why are liberals called left wing and conservatives right wing? This is a pentimento of pre-revolutionary France.

Do you know what a pentimento is? Neither did I until I looked it up. It's an underlying image in a painting, such as an earlier painting that shows through when the top layer of paint has worn with age.

It seems that in the National Assembly of France at the time the conservative nobility sat on the right hand side of the room and the reform-minded liberals sat on the left. The tags stuck.

Your pal has the wrong Tatum in mind

April 24, 2008

A friend of mine in the Scottsdale city government insists that Tatum Boulevard was named for Tatum O'Neal. I think this is proof that he must be drinking again because that just can't be true. Please help me out with this.

Well, I don't think you should be so quick to assume your friend is hitting the bottle again. Maybe he is just a bit confused. It happens.

But you are right: It just can't be true.

The boulevard is named for Russ F. Tatum, a real estate developer active around 1930 in the area around where the Paradise Valley Country stands today

Unfortunately for Tatum his timing was bad, and he lost his properties during the Depression.

OK, remember the question the other day from the lady who didn't like coyotes trotting through her neighborhood?

I offered up some lame idea about scaring them away with loud noises and asked if any of you people had any suggestions.

As usual, a few of you suggested shooting them.

Sigh.

But the great majority of you put forward the idea that I wish I had used in the first place—leave them alone.

In one way or another you people said the coyotes were there first, and as long as they're just passing through and not causing any problems they should left to go about their business.

I agree.

Over the past week I've watched a quail lay one or two eggs per day. Will they all hatch at the same time?

The eggs will hatch more or less synchronously, which means at the same time, and the chicks will be up and running within an hour of birth.

Did you know that male quail are pretty good fathers? While the female is on the nest the male stays nearby. And if the female should be killed before the eggs hatch, the male often takes over the incubation duties.

Just relax. You have a good gecko guest.

April 26, 2008

I had a small lizard walk into my house as I opened the door. Now what do I do? What do they eat? If it's a female could she be pregnant? And how many babies would she have? How long do they live? How big do they grow? If it dies would it smell? Help!

Geez, lady, relax. It's probably just a little gecko. It's not like you've got a komodo dragon in your house.

It's hard to say just what kind of gecko it is because there are 1,196 species worldwide, but I'd bet it's a Mediterranean house gecko. There are a lot of them around here. They're those little guys you see sunning themselves on the fence. They are about three inches long and come in a variety of colors—tan, yellow, pink or peach—and they have a bit of blue-green above each eye.

Actually, you should be happy to have it in the house. They eat crickets and cockroaches and spiders and the like. It's cheaper than hiring an exterminator.

Chances are you won't even see it again. They are most active at night, and it's probably found a snug cranny to use as its headquarters while it waits for a nice, juicy roach to come along. You might hear it chirping sometimes. Their name comes from the Malay word gekoq, which imitates the lizard's chirp.

I'd catch one myself and let it loose in the house, but the cat would probably think the lizard was there for its entertainment and not to catch bugs. And it might eat the spider that lives in my shower. We're buddies.

If it is a female she probably will lay two eggs two or three times a year. They sometimes eat the eggs before they hatch.

As for how long it will live, in the wild they have a lifespan of around five years, maybe longer. If yours is happy and safe and well-fed it could live as long as 10 years.

And as for your last question, I don't know. I've never stopped to smell a dead gecko. But I wouldn't think anything that small could give off much of a smell.

So just relax and be happy to have an on-site, all-natural bug-control service. Maybe you should give it a name. I call the spider in my shower Bob.

Cats' belly buttons and tumbleweeds

April 28, 2008

My wife said to write you to settle our argument. She says cats have navels. I said they don't, and to prove it I looked at our cat. The cat, of course, was not very cooperative, and I finally gave up after nursing a couple of scratches. So I guess it's up to you. Do cats have navels?

You people really don't have all that much to do, do you? I mean, have you looked around the house lately? Don't you think the baseboards might want dusting? Have you changed your oil on time?

Maybe you should go down to your neighborhood school and ask if they need some volunteer help. Somebody to listen to the kids read or help with the office work. Or there are all sorts of classes at your nearest community college.

But noooo. Not you people. You're just sitting around wondering if cats have belly buttons.

Pretty much all mammals—and that would include cats—that develop in the womb in amniotic sacs—and that would include cats—have navels.

They don't necessarily look like your belly button, be it an innie or an outie. It's more like a kind of scar under the cat's hair just south of the animal's rib cage.

Just leave it alone, OK? The cat isn't interested in letting you see it, and surely, as I said before, you must have something better to do.

I have always wondered about tumbleweeds. What were tumbleweeds before they became the stereotypical western prop rolling across the road?

Russian thistles.

They first showed up in the United States in South Dakota around 1877 in flax seed brought from the Ukraine. When the plant matures it breaks off at its base and is gone with the wind.

It is called a peregrinating plant. That means, "highly traveled." The tumbling action helps the plant scatter its seeds as it rolls along. There can be as many as 250,000 seeds per plant. So it is not too surprising that the thistle moved from South Dakota to the Pacific Coast by 1900.

You beat it to death with a cane?

May 14, 2008

My problem is an animal that looks like a toad that invaded the interior of my house. It was fat, soft, ugly as sin, hops like a toad but slowly. Gray in color, no or few warts. Googling didn't help me much. My mother never let me play with toads; I would get warts. But this creature must be a toad. Can you give me a name and attributes of its environment? The desert dryness seems extreme for frogs and toad. Would my garden pool be a breeding place? If so, the garden pool goes. Ugh. I have always been tolerant of any animal, but this thing was yucky. I had to beat it to death with my cane.

You beat it to death with your cane? Oh, for heaven's sake. What is it with you people always wanting to kill stuff just because it looks odd? I just don't know what I'm going to do with you people. Couldn't you just have shooed outside with a broom?

First of all you can't get warts from touching a toad. I can't believe any one actually believes that anymore.

Secondly, no, I can't tell you what kind of toad it was. There are lots of different kinds of toads in Arizona, including some that have adapted to life on the desert.

Third, could your garden pool be a breeding ground? Duh. Of course it could be. But surely you're not going to drain the pool just because you saw a toad? Think of all the mosquitoes the toads would eat.

There is only one toad in Arizona you need to worry much about—the Colorado River toad, also known as the Sonoran Desert toad.

This thing exudes a poison strong enough to kill a dog. And it does often turn up in dog water bowls. If your dog licks or picks up one of these toads you have to grab the hose and wash its mouth out as quickly as possible.

Our desert toads and frogs spend most of the year buried in the mud below seasonal ponds and washes.

When the monsoon rains come, they emerge for a couple of

frantic months of eating and mating and retreat underground again when things dry out.

Beat it to death with a cane. Sheesh.

You people.

Assorted matters

June 1, 2008

I got a phone message the other day from some guy in Glendale who wanted to know if the high-flying birds he sees over his house are vultures or condors.

I did not call him back to explain there are no condors in the Valley. It just seemed too silly.

And I got a message from a Phoenix woman who invited me to come over to her house to be dive-bombed by kestrels. Or at least she said they were kestrels.

I'm going to pass on that one. If I wanted to be pestered by small simple creatures I'd go down to the Black Tower and talk to my masters.

Two or three of you have called lately about the water-bag-and-flies thing. I don't know why. I guess it's the fly season.

Take small plastic bag, such as a sandwich bag, the kind you can pinch shut with your fingers. Fill it halfway with water and hang it out on your patio or wherever your fly problem is.

It does keep flies away, or at least it keeps my flies away. But nobody knows why for sure.

One idea is that it distorts their vision. Another is the flies mistake it for a hornets' nest. Flies don't like hornets

I was born with dark brown eyes. So dark that the hospital marked them down as black, but now they are hazel. They change between dark brown, hazel and green every day. Can you explain this? This is not at all uncommon. Many babies undergo a change in eye color during their first few years.

It happens as the eye is exposed to sunlight. This triggers the production of melanin pigment in the iris that gives you your adult eye color. As for your eyes going from brown to hazel to green or whatever, that's not too unusual, either. The color of your eyes is more about the reflection of the light around you then it is about the workings of your iris.

Your eye color can change a bit from the reflection of colors of the clothes you wear, from eye makeup, from stress or illness or from medications.

Hosing the roof to stay cool?

June 12, 2008

We have this neighbor who hoses down his roof several times a day. Since his roof can't be that dirty, we speculate that he may be trying to cool the roof down. However, we are rather skeptical that such a light spray of water would have a significant cooling effect. Could this be some old-timer secret for cooling the house in the hot Arizona summer?

It is indeed an old-timers' strategy for cooling off the house, but I don't know how well it works. But then one wants to be careful about arguing with old-timers. Some of them get cranky.

The idea is that the water on the roof will evaporate and thus will draw heat off the roof and the attic, thus cooling the house.

In theory that might be true, but I'm not sure just how much cooling would actually be achieved. Mostly because I am far too lazy to put a thermometer in my attic and then spray the roof and then see if it made in any difference.

To tell the truth, I'm not even sure I want to go up into my attic. I'm not sure what might be up there.

Also, this spraying-the-roof thing sounds like kind of a waste of water thing, compared to how much it might actually cool the house.

This guy must either have an evaporative cooler or an air conditioner. I suspect either would be more useful. Granted, the AC can be expensive to run, but if it were me I'd rather do that then hose down my house several times a day.

Or maybe he should get an attic fan.

On the other hand, it's his house and if he wants to spray it down with water I guess that's his business.

Did you know that back in the days before air conditioning or evaporative cooling people used to put big rocks on their roof during the summer?

I think they learned this trick from Native Americans, but I'm not sure.

The idea was that the rocks would heat up during the day and when it cooled at night the rocks would radiate heat away and in the process would draw heat from the house.

Disposing of old Scriptures

June 24, 2008

I recently was cleaning out a closet and found three old Bibles that are in very bad shape. What's the proper way to dispose of an old Bible? It seems sacrilegious just to throw them in the trash.

Are you sure they are no longer usable? If they are you could give them to a church or a jail or prison ministry.

If you are going to get rid of them, be sure you go through them carefully to make sure there aren't any old letters or pictures or whatever tucked between the pages.

Then you can either bury them or burn them.

Most Protestants wrap old Bibles in a white cloth and bury them. Roman Catholics either bury them or burn them. Some bury the ashes and some let them scatter to the winds.

Most Jewish synagogues have a storeroom called a genizah in which old scriptures and sacred writings that are too old for use are held until they are buried.

I'm pretty sure Muslims bury their unusable sacred writings, too.

I know you're squeamish about just tossing the Bibles out, but one could argue that putting them in the recycling bin would be an act of good stewardship of God's beautiful earth.

I have a question that's been bothering me for a few years. When birds bore holes in a saguaro cactus to build nests and have babies, why don't the eggs cook from the direct sunlight beaming on the cactus all day? How in the world can they take that heat?

Think about it for a minute: Birds have been nesting and raising their young in saguaro cavities for thousands and thousanda and thousands of years. If it were not a suitable environment for such things you would think the birds would have figured it out ages ago and found other places to nest.

Depending on which direction the cavity faces, the temperature inside can be about 10 degrees cooler than the outside air.

The eggs are at the bottom of the cavity and not in direct sunlight, and the cactus' thick walls provide insulation just like a thick adobe wall does.

Does the Colorado River keep Yuma dry?

June 28, 2008

I have heard that the reason why Yuma receives hardly any rain during the year is because of some type of electromagnetic field that emanates from the Colorado River and causes any cloud build-up to scatter over it. I tried looking on the National Oceanic and Atmospheric Administration website but couldn't find anything about it.

Huh?

It is true that flowing water can create an electromagnetic field. That might be why some people are able to dowse or water witch to find an underground source of water. It could be they are more sensitive to changes in electromagnetic fields than the rest of us are.

And it is true that turbid or muddy or salty water has a greater conductivity than clear, fresh water.

And it is true that it doesn't rain much in Yuma—around 3 inches a year.

But if the Colorado River were cranking out enough of an electromagnetic field to affect the weather it would truly be a miraculous kind of stream indeed.

Think about it: There are plenty of flowing streams all over the place where the surrounding areas get plenty of rain.

Yuma is so dry because, for among other reasons, it sits only 140 or so feet above sea level in a whopping great hot desert. It doesn't have anything to do with the Colorado.

Recently your newspaper printed a picture of a horse wearing a mask. I have seen this in the pastures around here, but never before moving to Arizona. Is this to protect the horse's eyes from the Arizona sun?

A horse facemask does help protect a horse's pink skin under white facial markings from the sun.

However, its main purpose is to protect the beast's face from gnats or biting flies or other annoying bugs. Some include flaps to keep bugs out of the ears.

A horse mask usually has a mesh covering over the eyes so the horse can still see. That mesh is raised a bit to leave room for the animal's eyelashes to work.

Termites or ants or whatever?

July 14, 2008

I have noticed many thin insect wings about half an inch long floating in my pool this time of year after a rain shower. Early Sunday evening, I noticed many flying insects attempting to fly through the raindrops. When the raindrops hit their bodies, they were forced to the ground. All over the cool deck were the same type of winged insects struggling to dry off, and I noticed they look like reddish-brown ants with wings. I say they must be termites. My husband says, "Whatever." Can you help with this identification?

They could be termites, I suppose, but I think it is more likely that they are flying ants.

Did you know that Arizona has more species of ants than any other state in the country? We have 318 species here. That's a lot.

It's probably because we have so many difference ecosystems, from desert to alpine and a lot of others in between.

Anyway, most ants in a colony are wingless, sterile females. However, around this time of year when the humidity is high and the rains come winged males and winged females take flight in great swarms.

They mate in the air and the males die soon afterwards.

The females go off to form a new colony and lose their wings. Why would you need wings if you spend almost your entire life underground?

Female flying ants are capable of storing sperm for many years. This helps them keep the colony populated. They can crank out fertilized or unfertilized eggs depending on whether the colony needs females or males.

Like I said, they might be termites. One way to tell the difference between ants and termites is the wings.

They both have four wings, but in termite the wings are the same length and in ants the two front wings are longer then the rear set.

And termite wings are twice as long as the body.

Another thing to look for is the waist. Ants have thin waists while termites have a chunky, broad-waisted look to them.

Cooking an egg on the sidewalk?

July 26, 2008

I have heard it said: "It is hot enough to cook an egg on the sidewalk." My question is: How hot does it actually have to be to cook an egg on the sidewalk, and is it better to use a small pan or a piece of aluminum foil?

A few years ago one of my masters came skulking around my cubicle—those were in the days when I wore pants and shirts and shoes and actually went into work at the Dark Tower every day—and suggested that I try to do that frying-an-egg-on-the-sidewalk thing.

Fortunately for me, I had a stapler and some sheets of paper at hand, and I showed him how the stapler worked and gave him the paper and he went off happy and lost interest in the egg venture.

Even after all this time when I am in the office I walk by his cubicle and there he is with the stapler and a stack of paper. He seems happy. Maybe I should show him the copy machine.

Anyway, I'm thinking that if it is hot enough to fry an egg on the sidewalk, it is too hot to be outside trying to fry an egg on the sidewalk.

Here's the deal: You need a surface temperature of around 158 degrees or so to warp the proteins in a raw egg enough to turn them into a cooked egg.

It has something to do with denaturing proteins, whatever that means.

And even if you could fry an egg on the sidewalk, who would want to eat it? Euww.

Now I'm not saying that if you sprayed some of that Pam stuff on some aluminum foil, with the edges curled up, and put it out on the sidewalk in the direct sunlight, and cracked an egg on it that the egg wouldn't cook.

But I am thinking it might take a while.

I don't know for sure, but you might be better off trying to fry an egg on the hood of your car, although you might want some extra insulation under the aluminum foil.

Otherwise, your spouse, parents, significant other, friend or neighbor might be a bit annoyed about the damage, if any, to the paint job caused by your short order cooking.

Your wife is right—get out of the pool

July 28, 2008

My wife and I are having a disagreement about whether it is safe to swim during a monsoon storm. She insists that I get out of the pool when the wind barely even is blowing because she's afraid I'll get electrocuted. I think I'm OK because otherwise fish would be dead. Who's right? It's worth a dinner to me if I am.

Umm, I have news for you, pal. The fish are dead.

When lightning strikes a lake or the ocean the charge tends to spread out along the surface until it dissipates. However, fish near the site of the strike or near the surface are either stunned or killed.

Your wife is right. A swimming pool is not a healthy place to be during a thunderstorm.

It's not just that lightning is attracted to water, and that water is a fairly good conductor of electricity. It's the fact that you are out in the open just like you were on a golf course or standing out in your yard.

And your pool is reinforced with metal rods under the concrete, and they could attract lightning, too.

Even if the bolt did not make a direct hit on your pool, a strike nearby could travel along the ground to nail you.

Your wife also is correct in urging you to leave the water at the first signs of the storm. Lightning can strike from as far as 10 miles away. So even if the storm looks like it's a long way off, you need to get out of the pool.

I don't think I have ever seen a baby pigeon, or for that matter, even one that was half-grown. I asked around, and no one else can recall seeing one, either. Do they just hang around the nest until they are full-grown?

For one thing, pigeons tend to hide their nests in places you are not likely to see them—the underside of bridges, for instance.

Secondly, pigeons are pretty good parents. Both the male and the female care for the young and they continue to do so until the squabs are fully feathered out.

When they do leave the nest they are so near in size and plumage to the adults around them that you really can't pick them out.

Controlling your air space

July 29, 2008

This has bugged me for several weeks now. How much air do I own above my property where I live? Would I own the air space 1 inch off the ground? If so, then how high does my space go?

Why in the world would this bother you so much? Don't you have any other things to worry about concerning your property? Like keeping the yard neat or painting the house or maintaining the sprinklers? I don't know about you, but my sprinklers are a great mystery to me. I think they were installed by Druids. You also have to worry about your air space?

Or are you afraid someone might inhale air that is legally yours?

What are you planning on doing? Shooting a surface-to-air missile at a passing helicopter? Using your BB gun on a neighborhood kid's kite? I wouldn't put that past some of you.

Geez, you people. Just relax. There is enough for everybody. You worry me a lot.

Here's the deal in a nutshell: the Federal Aviation Administration is in charge of controlling all air space in the United States. That includes setting rules and regulations, such as the one that says pilots, in most cases, have to keep their crafts 500 or 1,000 feet away from you or man-made structures, unless they are taking off or landing or cruising over your property to scope out the marijuana garden in your backyard for law enforcement purposes.

However, over the years the courts have ruled that your air space extends to the point that is "essential to the use and enjoyment of your land."

That means you can cut back the branches of your neighbor's trees that lap over the fence on to your side, or you can add an extra story to your house or you can put up a big antennae, zoning rules allowing, but you can't get out the old 12-gauge and fire away at passing planes.

Nor can you hope to collect trespassing fees from airlines whose planes fly over your home at high altitudes. I would be surprised if some of you people hadn't already thought about trying that.

Are you sure that scorpion in the pool is dead?

July 30, 2008

I found a scorpion in the bottom of our pool and we wondered if they could swim? Did it sink right away or swim around until it ran out of energy and drowned?

Did you know that around 400 million years ago there were creatures known as sea scorpions, ancestors of our present scorpions, that lived in the primeval seas and were as much as 8 feet long? *An 8-foot scorpion.* That would keep you awake at night.

Anyway, about the scorpion in your pool. Are you sure it was dead?

Scorpions often come to swimming pools for a drink of water, but I don't think they are built for swimming.

However, some varieties of scorpions can live under water for as long as 48 hours, just like some scorpions can go for as long as a year without eating.

They're tough.

So if you do find a scorpion in your pool, scoop it out without handling it. It might still be alive and well and somewhat aggrieved.

Do you know the history of using a pig for a savings bank, i.e., the piggy bank?

This goes back to 15th century England when people made jars and dishes and household stuff out of orange clay known as "pygg."

And if you happened to have an extra coin or two, you might put it in a jar made of pygg. Over time pygg came to sound like "pig" and some time in the 18th century some unknown inventive potter started making "pygg jars" in the shape, more or less, of a pig.

I am thinking of turning off my water heater for the summer to save on my gas bill. I bathe in cold water that's so hot it's almost too hot to shower in. I wash my clothes in cold water that's just as hot and I'm sure the dishwasher, with its built-in electric heater, could make up any temperature difference it needs, if any. So would it be a wise move to turn off my gas water heater during the summer?

It sounds like you've already made up your mind to do so. Drain the heater and make sure you cut off the gas supply completely so there aren't any leaks.

Geckoes, mosquitoes and the new moon

August 6, 2008

I have at hand a note from some guy whose wife accidentally stepped on and squished a gecko. He wants to know if anyone keeps statistics on how often such things happen.

You people. Who in the world would keep numbers on squished geckos?

Let's do this one instead.

Is it true that wolves are the natural enemies of coyotes and that if a pack of wolves finds a lone coyote they will kill it and if a pack of coyotes finds a lone wolf they will kill it?

Yes, the two species hate each other.

That's one reason coyote populations are booming—the wolves are mostly gone.

One point: Coyotes don't form structured packs like wolves do. A group of coyotes is usually made up of two or three siblings or just a male and female.

How long do mosquitoes live?

It depends on a bunch of things.

Male mosquitoes generally live a week or so and don't go very far from the site where they were born.

Females—the blood suckers—live any where from three weeks to two or three months and will travel several miles looking for a blood meal.

Temperature, humidity, the food supply and the season of the year are all factors in the life span.

During her life a female will lay several hundred eggs in batches of 50 or 100 or so.

I know that the second full moon in the same month is called a blue moon. What about the second new moon in a month? What is that called?

Not much of anything as far as I can tell. The odds of two new moons in the same month are the same as the odds for two full moons. However, since the new moon isn't as showy as a full moon it usually goes unnoticed and doesn't seem to have any special name.

I did determine the Wiccans call a second new moon the black moon.

Spells cast under a black moon are said to be especially powerful.

Caterpillars on the move

August 23, 2008

I have a question my wife asked me to write to you about. It seems that on her drive to and from work, she sees these white or pale yellow worms about 1.5 to 2 inches long crossing the Interstate 10, both east to west and west to east. It looks like they are in a crosswalk, as they spread approximately 3 feet wide. She has also seen them on Riggs Road west of Sun Lakes. She is wondering what kind of worm or whatever they may be.

Your wife is not alone in wondering about this. Others among you people have called or written about this in the past few days.

This phenomenon looks kind of creepy, but it is completely harmless.

It is a migration of caterpillars—the larvae of the white-lined sphinx moth. Every year about this time they pick up and move in great masses.

They can be anything from yellow and green with black dots or stripes to black with just a bit of yellow. They have a prominent horn-like thing toward the rear of the body. When threatened or scared they rear up their heads, trying to look tough and sometimes spit out a thick green liquid. They aren't poisonous, so don't worry about them.

Just why they set off on these migrations isn't quite clear, according to Carl Olson, the University of Arizona bug man. One idea is that they are looking for more suitable soil to dig into to pupate—turn into the adult moth. Or maybe they have just depleted the sources of food in their old neighborhood.

And nobody knows how they decide where they're going or if they follow the same routes every year or why they might pick one neighborhood over another. If they do pick your neighborhood, I wouldn't worry about it too much. They probably won't eat that much.

The Tohono Oldham used to scoop them up, dry them and eat them.

The adult moth is a handsome thing, as moths go, with wing-span of about 5 inches.

You can see a picture of the adult moth and its caterpillars at www.desertusa.com. Click on "Animals," then "Insects & Spiders," and then look under "Flying Insects."

Which animals can or can't swim

September 4, 2008

My grandson and I made a wager about which (if any) animals cannot swim. A lot rides on your answer, mainly his picking up the dog poop in my back yard.

I don't know from your note which side you took in this matter. So you may or may not have to pick up the dog poop yourself.

I don't know that I have ever seen a chicken swim, but then I am a shy and retiring young thing and don't get out much, so I have to say I don't know if I have ever had an opportunity to see a chicken swim. Nor can I imagine the circumstances under which such an opportunity might arise.

The results of the research I did on this matter before it was time for a nap were mixed. I'm not sure what I believe.

I am reliably told that hippos, even though they are aquatic animals, can't swim very well, if at all, and mostly just trudge along on the bottom of a stream waiting to bite people, which they seem to do with some frequency. And I guess giraffes aren't much for the water.

And I am told that some gorillas and orangutans can't swim because their centers of gravity are too high. I know the feeling, except I'm afraid mine is too low.

One thing I read said that camels can't swim, but then another piece said racing camels in Dubai regularly exercise in camel swimming pools, although it seems they have to be coaxed a bit to get in.

Elephants are good swimmers. Apparently there are islands in the Indian Ocean that have been populated by elephants that swam some distance from the mainland to get there. Why they chose to do this, I don't know.

I also read that bats can swim. That's interesting, don't you think? I wonder when bats would have occasion to swim.

Actually, it's a wonder that people can swim. Many primates have faces and noses that jut forward in a manner that would let them swim and get a breath at the same time, sort of like dog paddling. But people mostly have to turn their heads to the side to catch a breath if they are swimming properly. This is why some of us stick to side-stroking.

Returning kidneys doesn't work

September 18, 2008

Maybe you can settle a question my friend and I are debating: If you need a kidney transplant and one of your children steps up and donates one of theirs, then you die could that kidney be transplanted back into them?

What do you mean "maybe?" Of course I can answer your question.

I can answer your question because I called my new best pals at Banner Health, and they put me in touch with Dr. Alfredo Fabrega, and he knew all about stuff like this. That's good because he is the medical director for Banner Transplant Services, so you kind of would expect he'd know all about this.

Anyway, he said returning a kidney to the donor is not possible or recommended.

For one thing, the original donor must have been healthy enough to get by with one kidney or he or she wouldn't have been allowed to donate in the first place.

"To subject him to another surgery to retransplant the organ back into him puts him through a large and needless surgery with all the associated risks and recovery time. In addition, he may be exposed to any infections the original transplant recipient may have had," Fabrega wrote in an e-mail.

Next, when the organ is transplanted there is significant scarring around it that would make it very difficult to remove and still be in good condition to retransplant.

And by the time initial transplant recipient dies, there is usually organ damage that would make the organ unsuitable for retransplanting.

However, Fabrega said there have been rare cases in which a patient died very soon after the transplant and the organ was removed and given to another patient who needed a kidney.

How high can a bird fly without ill effects?

It depends on the bird.

According to the Audubon Society, bar-headed geese migrate over Mount Everest and that's 29,028 feet.

The record goes to an unlucky Ruppell's griffon, a kind of vulture. In 1975 it got sucked into a jet engine 37,900 feet over the Ivory Coast. The plane was damaged, but landed safely. The griffon didn't.

Aha! That's it

September 24, 2008

The other day I was working on a hard crossword puzzle and finally got stuck on one last word. I worked on it several more minutes and finally gave up and put the puzzle aside. As soon as I did, the answer popped into my mind. This has happened to me before. How does this work?

That happens to me, too. Especially in the shower. I have a lot of good ideas in the shower, or at least ideas that seem pretty good at the time.

I think this happens to pretty much everybody. It's kind of weird, huh?

It took a while, but I finally found the answer in *Psychology: the Adaptive Mind*, a textbook by James Nairne of Purdue University, who is, not surprisingly, a professor of psychology.

According to Nairne, psychologists call this phenomenon the incubation effect. Nobody seems to know for certain how it works.

One idea is that after you and the conscious part of your brain go off to do something else, such as cleaning the bedroom closet or making a liverwurst sandwich or walking around the block, the unconscious part of your brain is still working on the problem.

And without you and the awake part of your brain around to annoy it, it comes up with the answer.

Another idea is that you have just been thinking and thinking about this problem in the wrong way over and over again and getting more and more wrong about it.

So when you give up on it your brain kind of gives a sigh of relief and punches its reset button and goes at it from another, and rewarding, direction.

One more idea is that when you turn your attention to some other matter, whatever that matter might be, that matter gives your brain a clue or a hint to your original unsolved problem and your brain slaps your hand to your forehead and makes you say, "Aha! That's it."

There might have been another explanation, but I can't think of it just now. Maybe I should go take a shower.

Hurricanes in Arizona

October 12, 2008

Does the Gulf of California have enough water mass to sustain a hurricane up the middle all the way from its tip to Arizona?

Sort of, but such an event is very rare.

According to the National Weather Service, in late August and early September of 1967 Hurricane Katrina crossed the tip of Baja California and bounced its way up the Gulf of California toward Yuma.

Along the way it destroyed dozens of boats and about half the town of San Felipe in Baja Norte.

It came to land at the mouth of the Colorado River, but it was weakened by the mountains on either of side of the Gulf and hit Arizona as a tropical depression. Two to 4 inches of rain fell across southwest Arizona before the storm wore itself out.

Arizona's worst hurricane-related storm came on Labor Day 1970 when the remains of tropical storm Norma hit central Arizona.

Twenty-three people were killed, including 14 who drowned in flash floods on Tonto Creek near Kohl's Ranch.

At Workman Creek north of Globe 11.4 inches of rain fell in 24 hours.

I am paranoid about lizards about any kind. I have been killing baby lizards in my condo for weeks now. I've killed six, and have seen one move faster than I could react. The exterminators who handle our condo work do not have any ideas for me. Do you?

Well, yes I do, but you probably won't like it. I think you should try to relax and stopping killing them. They're not going to hurt you, and they eat bugs.

Try trapping a lizard under a plastic cup. Slide a sheet of paper under the cup to trap it and release the critter outside in peace.

The shape of rabbit things yet to come

October 16, 2008

My family was observing the bunnies at the State Fair and noticed that their deposits were almost perfectly round. Can you explain?

So it's come down to this.

After a perfectly rotten day of dogs rolling around in dead grass and then shaking it off all over the living room floor all day; of dealing with a sprinkler system infested with demons whose name is Legion; of dealing with a brand new computer that seems to be in cahoots with the sprinkler demons, it has come to this: The shape of rabbit poop.

Sigh.

I suppose my mother would have told me there would be days like this if she had ever even dreamed there would be days like this.

Anyway, God help me, I actually put some effort into this one and came up empty. The only thing I can think of is that the pellets are shaped by the shape of rabbits' large intestine, which I suppose must be round. I haven't looked.

Now as long as we are on this topic, I did learn something.

Rabbits have two kind of excrement. The round, dry ones and another kind that looks sort of like mulberries called cecotropes, which the bunny eats.

Don't ask me why. I am sure there is a perfectly good reason, but I neither know why nor feel inclined to find out why this should be so.

Anyway, the nice small round ones are a good source of nitrogen and can be dug into your garden or flowerbeds without composting them first.

But here's what bothers me about this question: You went to the State Fair. The fair is full of many odd and interesting things and maybe even educational things, and you came away wondering about rabbit poop?

You people.

No need for warming up

October 20, 2008

A family member is driving us crazy. She insists that anyone who drives her car must warm it up for five minutes. She has a 2003 Volkswagen Jetta. We tell her that only applies to the old cars, not the newer models. She lectures us anytime we drive her car and we are ready to run over her. Please hurry and verify that we are right and she is bonkers.

She is bonkers, but I don't think you should run over her. That seems a bit harsh. I mean if we just went around running over everybody we thought was bonkers there would hardly be any of us left.

Modern fuel-injected cars do not need a warm-up session when you start up.

Now if you lived in a very cold climate it might be wise to let the car warm a bit to get the oil flowing and get the passenger compartment warm.

Assuming your relative does not live somewhere with frigid weather, all she is doing is wasting gasoline and adding to the Brown Cloud.

How does my nose know it's morning? In the morning my nose runs, but not during the night or during the day. But when I get up in the morning, it runs and I need to blow it. Just how smart is a nose, and why would it choose to run first thing in the morning?

Gee, I don't know if your nose is any more or less smart than, say, your bellybutton.

It is a simple matter of gravity.

When you are in bed, horizontal, the mucus drains to the back of your throat and you swallow it in your sleep.

When you are awake and vertical it drains out of your nose and you have to give it a good honk.

Why your nose only runs when you first wake up and not during the rest of the day I am not sure. I suppose it just need to drain out a bit.

Power of attorney doesn't let you vote

October 24, 2008

I've just had to put my husband in a nursing home. He has severe Alzheimer's. I have his power of attorney. My question is can I cast his vote from him in the election? He always voted a straight Democratic ticket.

First of all, let me say I am sorry to hear about your husband. That must be very hard on you, and I hope you remember to take care of yourself.

Next, I'm afraid the power of attorney doesn't allow you to vote for him.

Arizona law—Title 16-1029—says this: "A power of attorney or other form of proxy is not valid for use by a person in any procedure or transaction concerning elections, including voter registration, petition circulation or signature, voter registration cancellation, early ballot requests or voting another person's ballot."

I suppose if you had a mail-in ballot you could fill it out for your husband, but he would have to sign in.

And the deadline for asking for a mail-in ballot is now past.

I have read there are times when you can see the Space Station from Earth. About twilight some months ago, I saw a bright object cross the sky at incredible speed. An airliner was up there at the same time, dragging a contrail. The object, certainly much higher, had no contrail. Could that object have been the Space Station?

Probably, but it's hard to say for sure.

If you remembered the exact date I might be able to go back and figure it out, but that sounds like a lot of work.

You can find a daily schedule of when the International Space Station is visible at www.heavens-above.com.

Click on ISS.

A schedule of sightings for the week ahead also runs with the astronomy chart on Saturdays in *The Republic*.

The real dirt on all that grimy stuff covering things

October 30, 2008

I recently saw a show about Jamestown on PBS. All the archaeological sites shown were buried. My question is: Where does the dirt come from? How does it get there?

What do you mean, where does dirt come from? It's dirt. It's just there.

This is perhaps a sort of simple example, but think for a minute about how much dust can build up on furniture in your otherwise clean and tidy house if you're gone for a couple of weeks or if you just don't get around to dusting for a while. Multiply that by centuries, and pretty soon you're talking about a lot of dirt.

The Earth's surface is not a static, unchanging thing. It shifts and slides and moves around. Winds, erosion, changing climates, volcanoes, human activity and all sorts of things account for a shifting surface. For instance, over the centuries, shifting sands buried many of Egypt's pyramids and partly covered up the Sphinx.

I saw that PBS thing on Jamestown, too. What did they spend a lot of time excavating? Graves and pilings for building foundations and so on. In other words, they were digging up stuff that was buried to begin with.

It's the same with garbage dumps and middens, which are rich sources for archaeological finds. They were already buried before time began to add to the cover.

Another thing: Archaeologists digging up ancient towns usually find various layers of older cities underneath. When a city was knocked out by war or disease or whatever, the new people tended to build on top of whatever was there before.

There also is the fact that Earth picks up a few thousand tons of space dust every year, but not so much that it would account for covering up ancient civilizations.

Keep cats away from tarantula

November 1, 2008

Having recently moved here and having purchased a home site around Happy Jack I have seen a few tarantulas while clearing brush. After a little research I am not too concerned for myself. I plan not to bother them so they won't bother me. And it appears that their bites are not too bad, but wasp-like. However, I wonder how toxic a bite would be to my Siamese cats. They will surely chase a large bug. Also, somebody told me that there is a plant that they do not like and will keep them away. I could not find any information on this, so I am inclined to disbelieve it, but it never hurts to check.

Tarantulas around Happy Jack? That's at about 7,500 feet. That strikes me as kind of high for tarantulas, but I'll take your word for it.

Anyway, I am going to rule in favor of the tarantulas on this one.

It is true that a tarantula bite won't hurt you much more than a bee sting. But it also is true that a tarantula bite could cause swelling or perhaps anaphylactic shock in a cat or dog.

I did read one thing that said a mixture of pipe or chewing tobacco boiled in a gallon of water, strained and mixed with some lemon-scented dish soap will keep spiders away.

But let us consider it this way.

The last time I checked Siamese cats are not native to the ecosystem around here and shouldn't be roaming around outside terrorizing birds and tarantulas or whatever else they come across. Keep them inside and let them doze on sunny windowsills.

The tarantulas were there before you and the cats showed up.

Keep the cats inside and leave the tarantulas alone. And enjoy your new home. It's nice up there.

Alpha stage of sleep can feel like you're awake

November 11, 2008

Sometimes when I'm lying in front of the TV I will close my eyes and believe that I am completely awake. I'm sure I can still hear the TV and/or have thoughts of my day running through my head. However, my wife often tells me that during these periods I am snoring very loudly. How can I be snoring and obviously asleep while I think I am still awake and at least listening to the TV?

When my daughters were little if I fell asleep watching TV they would have long conversations with me and then wake me up to report all of the things I said in my sleep. They thought this was hilarious.

Anyway, I think what's happening is that you are going through the alpha stage of sleep, the first of four stages of non-REM sleep.

During the alpha stage your brain waves slow down to about eight to 12 cycles per second. Your breathing slows, your blood pressure falls, and the flow of blood to your brain decreases.

And in your case, your head probably slumps forward a bit and certain muscles in your respiratory system relax and you snore.

But your brain still remains fairly active while you're asleep, so it might still be processing sounds from the TV. Or you are dreaming that you are still listening to some show.

Many people who are awakened during the alpha stage claim they hadn't been asleep at all. They were just resting their eyes.

I was wondering if there is any difference between an earthquake and a temblor. The two words seem to be used interchangeably by the media.

They are used interchangeably because they are the same thing. An earthquake is a temblor and a temblor is an earthquake.

You may think I'm a hack, but I an old cowpuncher

November 18, 2008

So, I just wandered out to get the mail, hoping none of my neighbors would notice I was still in my jammies at that time of day, and found, among other stuff, a catalog from the National Roping Society and one from another outfit selling a lot of Western stuff.

I get such things every now and then because the guy who owned my house two or three owners back was a saddle maker, and his tidy workshop is now my messy storeroom. There is a picture out there of him at a rodeo.

So did I toss out these too-early Christmas catalogs that have nothing to do with me?

Smile when you say that, pardner. I read every page of every one of them.

Do I need a DVD on goat roping? Well, not really, but what the heck. I especially liked the ladies' T-shirt with the slogan: Farm Girl: Ain't Afraid To Get Dirty.

Many of you might suppose that I am just an oafish Midwest farm boy who happened to stumble into newspaper work.

Truth be told, I ride an old paint and I lead an old dam and I'm going to Montana to throw a hoolihan.

I am actually a nephew of the Cisco Kid. I had a tragic love affair with Dale Evans. Ben Johnson was my grandfather. Or maybe it was one of those guys from Lonesome Dove.

Sorry, but I've been living a lie all these years. I've been answering your questions and making snarky comments and cheap jokes when my true destiny really has been to strap on my Colts, hang up my Wyoming cattle-brand shower curtain, cover my Kleenex with a wild horses boutique tissue box and saddle up my pony using my special Marlene McRae cinch. I have no idea who Marlene McRae is or was, but what the heck.

Yipee-ty-yi-o.

Where's Joseph?

November 28, 2008

Why is there no Joseph statue in my tabletop Nativity set? Is this some kind of a Catholic thing?

Well, I don't think this is necessarily a Roman Catholic thing.

But first we have to talk about a timing thing. What are you doing messing around with your crech, your Nativity scene now? Huh?

Everyone knows—or at least I have just always assumed that everybody knows—that you can't get out your creche, or wreath or tree or Christmas lights or inflatable Santas or whatever until after Dec. 13. That's my older daughter's birthday. No Christmas until after that. That's the rule.

Without rules, what do we have? Anarchy. That's what.

I'm always surprised how many of you people don't understand that.

As long as we're on the subject: Those inflatable Santas and other inflatable holiday things—I really hate those. But to each their own.

Anyway, about Joseph.

The story goes that he was engaged to Mary and then found out before they were married that she was preggers and in a way that hadn't required his participation.

So Joseph decided to call the whole thing off until an angel came to him in a dream and told him to marry her anyway. Which, we are told, he did.

Nonetheless, poor old Joseph still gets dropped from some traditional Nativity scenes because he was a bit hinky at first about taking for his wife a woman who was already in a family way.

I'm not sure how fair that is to Joseph, because he did come through and did the right thing after all. And just now I can't remember if my own Nativity set includes him. I can't look at it until after Dec. 13.

Old guy in bathrobe' rises to occasion despite snub

December 5, 2008

I don't feel so hot. I've had a bad day. My digestive system is in rebellion. I don't know if I just feel stressed or if I'm coming down with something or if it was that pickled herring I found in the back of the refrigerator.

That's pretty impressive whining, don't you think? I'm pretty good at whining, but this might be one of my best. I guess I'll just knock this out and have a bowl of nature's most perfect cure—chicken noodle soup. Then I'll feel better.

So let's get at it.

My boyfriend and I were talking politics recently and the term "blue dog Democrat" was used. When neither of us could come up with the origin of the term, my boyfriend said "Why don't you write to 'the old guy in the bathrobe' and ask him?"

The old guy in the bathrobe? I'm not sure what I think about that. Oh, well.

A blue dog Democrat is one who is open to some conservative ideas.

After the Civil War the states of the defeated South were solidly Democratic for many decades.

In 1928 the Democratic presidential nominee was a northerner and a Roman Catholic—Al Smith. This did not sit well with Southern Democrats. But most of them stayed with the party. Their motto was "I'd vote for a yellow dog if he ran on the Democratic ticket."

Why a yellow dog? I don't know.

In 1994 a group of sort of conservative Democrats formed what they called the Blue Dog Coalition and tended to side with Republican on fiscal matters.

The name came from then-Rep. Pete Geren, a Texas Democrat who said the coalition's members had been "choked blue" by their more liberal colleagues. I learned all this at http://wordcraft.infopop.cc.

Why you have never seen a green mammal

December 17, 2008

There are green fish, green reptiles, green birds, green amphibians and green insects. Many space aliens are even reported to be green. I don't recall ever seeing a green mammal or even hearing about one. Are there any? If not, why not? If there are, why are they so rare? I think maybe I did this one a long time ago, but I'm too lazy to go back and look it up. And, besides, it's a good question.

Well, you'd look pretty silly if you were green, wouldn't you?

Actually, nobody knows for sure mammals don't come in green.

Mandrills have very colorful faces, including some flashes of green. Some mammals come with different colored stripes that can blend and make them look sort of olive green. And some sloths are so slothful that green algae grow in their hair and give a greenish look.

Pangolins are mammals whose hair over the centuries has turned sort of scale-like. Under certain light, those scales can look green.

Here's one idea: When the first mammals emerged on to the tree of life, millions of years ago, they were tiny little things that spent a lot of time scurrying around on the forest floor with its dead vegetation and dirt and so. And many still do today. Being green would make them stand out against the dull background, making them easy pickings for predators. It is true that many green insects live in similar situations, but they're a lot smaller and can find cover more easily.

Another thing: Most, but not all, of the animals that prey on mammals are other mammals.

Mammals, for the most part, have poor color vision.

So, why help them overcome that handicap by standing out in nice bright green?

Or maybe God just thought people and other mammals didn't look good in green.

What if the ex-president refuses to leave the White House?

January 6, 2009

What would happen if the outgoing president refused to move out of the White House at the end of his term? Would he get 10-, five- or three-day notices? Who would be responsible for getting him out?

Now that's a pretty interesting question, don't you think? It has never happened, of course, but it's kind of fun to imagine such a scenario. I suppose the U.S. marshals would have to go in and root the sore loser out.

The closest we've come to such a situation was in 1881 when Chester Arthur refused to move in to the White House until it was redecorated. I guess he didn't care much for the décor.

In the elections of 1916, Arizona's first governor, George W.P. Hunt, contested the results that showed him losing by 30 votes and refused to give up his office, leaving his challenger to work out of his home.

Hunt finally turned over the keys after the state Supreme Court ruled against him in 1917. Hunt was a stubborn man, though, and kept up his fight until later that year when the courts finally declared him the winner.

In some years the grapefruit off my neighbor's tree, and now my own tree, has very thick skins and other years it is very thin. Why? Also, fruit off the same tree yields fruit that is very tart and some that is not so tart.

A nice, smooth, unwrinkled skin on a grapefruit is a sign the tree was well watered and the fruit is full of juice.

When the skin is all wrinkled you can expect a dry, tart pulp, and remind yourself to give the tree bit more water next year.

As to why you're getting tart and not-so-tart fruit off the same tree, it could be a matter of uneven ripening.

Thermometer may read 36, but don't let that fool you

January 11, 2009

If water freezes at 32 degrees, how does frost form when the temperature is 36 degrees?

Easy. The temperature your thermometer shows is not necessarily the same as the temperature where the frost is forming.

Your thermometer probably is four or five feet or so above the ground and tells you at that height what the temperature is—say, 36.

However, on cool, calm nights, cold air, being denser than warm air, settles on the ground or in low places or perhaps on your roof or car top, where warmer air has been easily radiated away over night.

And it may well be in those places that the temperature is cold enough to allow frost to form, no matter what your thermometer tells you is going on just a few feet higher.

What is that rain that doesn't fall out of the sky? I know it starts with a "v."

You're thinking of virga. That's raindrops or snowflakes that fall from a cloud and evaporate well before they hit the ground.

Virga comes from the Latin word for "twig."

If a person has been sending Christmas cards to someone for years, and wants to stop sending them, what is the best way to proceed? Just stop sending the cards, or write a note explaining what you are doing so they'll know what's happening?

Gee, I don't know.

Do you mean you don't want to send out any cards at all or just cut some of the more marginal names from your list?

If you're giving it up all together, you might send a sort of general-purpose note to your friends this summer explaining your decision.

If you are just going to cull a bit, I wouldn't worry about it. Those people probably don't want to send you a card, either.

Do cat's colors tell us anything?

January 19, 2009

Have you been wrestling with your computer all day and at some point pulled out all those blue cords from various places and then plugged them in again and it still doesn't work?

If so you need Thompson's Tuesday Tech Tip brought to you by Valley 101, your full-service column.

The answer to your situation is that you have to plug the cords back into the same jack you took them out of. If you don't you'll have to go back and just keep sticking them in at random until the computer works, which can take some time depending on how many cords you unplugged and how tangled the whole pile is.

Always glad to help.

My wife and I have had many cats in 37 years of marriage. It seems that it is always the black ones that are most demanding of affection and meow the most to get what they want. Is this true of black cats in general?

You can't really predict a cat's personality by the color of its fur any more than you can tell what people will be like by the color of their hair.

I mean, "dumb blonde" and "fiery redhead" are not particularly reliable guideposts on the road of life, are they?

That said there are a few broad generalizations you can make in this matter. For instance, all-white cats may tend to be unfriendly because they often carry genes for blindness or deafness. Gray cats are said to be docile. But even stuff like that isn't always true.

One thing I read said black cats are more closely related to their wild ancestors than other cats. The idea is that being black made them harder to see so they were among the last to be domesticated.

Thus, black cats are said to be good hunters and if allowed to roam go farther than other cats. No word on them being unusually loud or affectionate.

A bodacious question

January 21, 2009

Several times recently I have heard "bodacious" used to imply something bold and audacious.

Internet sources I checked trace the word to the 1800s and say the meaning and source are unknown. One link mentioned the Iceni, a small tribe in East Anglia whose queen's name was Bouddica. She led her tribe to pillage London and other Roman settlements and probably helped Rome to leave British soil to the Brits. Is this the true source of the meaning of the word "bodacious"?

Actually, you got it right in your first sentence—bold and audacious.

According to several things I read, "bodacious" came out of the South in the 1930s where folks combined the words bold and audacious to create a word that meant "remarkable or prodigious."

It was popularized in the old comic strip Snuffy Smith, which has been running in newspapers around the world for a bodacious 90 years.

The word kind of fell out of use until 1982, when a character in An Officer and a Gentleman used it to describe portions of a young lady's upper body area.

The British queen you mentioned was Boudicca (or one of several other spellings), who led a revolt against the Romans after they strong-armed control of her Iceni tribe. During the power grab, the queen was beaten and her daughters raped.

Justifiably annoyed, Boudicca led a revolt that killed thousands of Romans and left many of their towns in ruins.

She died in battle around A.D. 60 either at the hand of an enemy or by poison.

She did not exactly drive the Roman invaders from British soil.

The last Roman troops left around A.D. 400.

The truth about "false dawns" and brown pelicans

January 25, 2009

I have been out and about very early in the morning many times but have never seen what the novelists used to refer to as the "false dawn," a period when the sky is said to lighten up for a time then go dark again before the actual dawn. Is there such a phenomenon?

Is there such a phenomenon? Sure, didn't you ever read *The Rubiayat* by Omar Khayyam?

"Before the phantom of false morning died / methought a voice within the tavern cried/ "When all the temple is prepared within/ Why lags the drowsy worshiper outside?"

Nice, huh? A little poetry always classes the place up a bit, doesn't it?

A false dawn is officially known as "zodiacal light" and usually occurs in the late summer or early autumn at mid- to upper-northern latitudes.

I don't know if mid-northern includes the Valley, but if Omar Khayyam could see the lights, I don't know why we couldn't.

Anyway, false lights are usually seen about two hours before true dawn. It looks, I am told, like a pyramid of light shooting up from the eastern horizon. Or did you ever drive out in the country at night and see the lights of a big city glowing on the horizon? A false dawn looks like that.

What you are seeing is sunlight reflected off tiny grains in a vast interplanetary dust cloud moving around the solar system.

There is a brown pelican living at the lakes around Glendale eating lots of fish. Does it need the saltwater of the ocean to live?

It will be fine. Brown pelicans are primarily saltwater birds, but a few of them turn up around here every year and, for the most part, seem no worse for the wear.

Cat years and human years

February 13, 2009

I have two cats. One is 13 calendar years old the other will soon be eight calendar years. The older one behaves the same way as the younger one. Should they be acting the same when there is five years difference in their ages?

Well, they're cats, aren't they? They're going to behave however they darn well want.

I guess the question is how much difference there is between eight and 13 in cat years.

If you work at it hard enough, which I certainly didn't, you can find all sorts of charts and formulas for converting human years to cat years.

The average lifespan for a housecat is about 15 years. The average lifespan for a human, at least in first world countries, is about 75 years. So you could say a cat year is about the same as five human years. But there is more to it than that.

For starters, a cat is a grown-up—physically and sexually—at one year of age. People are pretty much physically and sexually mature at around 15. (Emotional and intellectual maturity are a different matter.) So a one-year-old cat is more or less 15 in human years.

Next, most the charts show that at two years of age a cat has the same maturity levels of a 25-year-old human, although they still can't drive a car or buy a beer.

After that the averages seem to come out as one cat year per four people years.

That would make your 13-year-old fur ball about 69 and your eight-year-old 49. Should that make a difference in their behavior?

Let's face it: There are only so many things a cat can do—sleep, eat, maybe play a bit and then go back to sleep. So I wouldn't think 20 years would make all that much difference in the way they carry on.

The numbers say sunshine a good possibility in Valley

February 18, 2009

We are visiting from Chicago for two months. Here is our question: The Phoenix/Scottsdale area advertises 330 days of sunshine a year, and we want to know how it is calculated. If the sun breaks through the clouds for only 15 minutes one day, does that qualify?

Do you have any idea how much weight I've lost since I was in the hospital a while ago?

Well, it's none of your business. Don't be so nosey. Let's just say I feel like a jet.

Anyway, this is a pretty good question, don't you think? Especially since we are coming up on the very best time of the year—springtime in the Valley.

So, not to over-simplify, but the folks are at the National Weather Service look at the sky every day, and on a scale of 0 to 10 they decide how much of it they can see.

If the cloud cover is 0 to 3, it is considered to be a clear day. Four to 7 means it's partly cloudy and 8 to 10 is a cloudy day.

According to the record books, Yuma leads the nation in the number of clear days per year with 242 Phoenix is second with 211.

Pittsburgh and Caribou, Maine, tied for last with just 59 clear days per year. That must get you down after a while.

"Possible sunshine" is the total time that sunshine reaches the surface of Earth as the percentage of the maximum amount possible from sunrise to sunset with clear sky conditions

Yuma wins again in this regard, soaking up 90 percent of the sunshine it could possibly receive. Las Vegas and Phoenix tied for second with 85 percent. Portland, Ore., was last with just 48 percent.

As for Chicago, it gets 84 sunny days per year.

So snowbirds, in the words of the immortal Janis Joplin, "Get it while you can."

Some butt-lifting exercises (not that you need them)

February 23, 2009

There was an article in your newspaper Sunday that mentioned "Jane Fonda butt lifts" as part of an exercise routine. Would you please tell your readers, such as my wife, how to do this exercise?

Let me get this straight.

Are you suggesting that I somehow participate in a scheme to tell your wife her butt is too big?

Not on your life, pal. My mother didn't raise any dummies, although just between you and me I wonder about my brother sometimes.

So you're on your own on this one.

However, because I am feeling mildly magnanimous today, I'll give you a plan: Do the exercises yourself. I bet you need them anyway. When your wife notices and asks about it, just say you thought your rear could use a bit of work. In no way suggest that her own posterior ain't what it used to be. Hope that she will be inspired by your example.

So, here are a few exercises that will get you started.

First of all, a good brisk daily walk will do wonders not just for your butt, but for the rest of you, too. Ask the missus to come along because you'll miss her so if you go alone.

Get on your hands and knees. Lift one leg up and straight back behind you with your foot flexed, and bounce it a bit. Do this 10 times and then do the other leg. Three sets of 10 per leg. Or from the same position tuck a light weight behind your knee and lift your bent leg.

Standing leg lifts: Stand next to a wall. Stretch one hand out and push your palm against the wall. Lift the leg away from the wall out to the side. Flex the foot and lift the leg as far up as you can without moving your upper body. Do a bunch with one leg and then the other.

But leave me out of it, OK?

The law isn't picky about growing cotton

February 27, 2009

I have been wanting to grow a couple of pima cotton plants ever since a lengthy article about it appeared in the paper some time ago. Any clue where I might start hunting? Or maybe such things are not available to the public.

Why this guy wants to grow a couple of cotton plants, I don't know. Maybe they make attractive patio plants or maybe he's just curious or maybe he wants to weave his own clothes. I just read that you can make 1,200 pillowcases from one 480-pound bale of cotton. That's a lot of pillowcases.

Anyway, by "such things" I assume he means cotton seeds. Why wouldn't they be available to the public? That wouldn't make any sense. It's not like cotton seeds are a controlled substance or some tightly guarded agricultural secret. Production of colored cotton, however, is closely regulated, so stick with white.

I turned to Google and typed in a few appropriate keywords and found a bunch of seed catalogs and some local stores that stock cotton seeds in manageable amounts. Plus, you might check out the ads in various organic-gardening magazines or Web sites.

As for actually growing the stuff, I am told it loves warm weather and needs at least six hours of direct sunlight daily. Planting basil close by will help keep insects away.

Be careful not to over-water, it, especially when the bolls mature. They should be ready in about 120 days or so. One thing I read said you should treat ornamental cotton like you would treat patio tomatoes. Of course, I never seem to have any luck with patio tomatoes, so I guess I'll pass on the cotton thing.

Good luck. Let me know what happens. Send me a pillowcase.

Older gents, fluff up those bushy eyebrows with pride

March 6, 2009

Now that the temperatures are going up we're starting to see fence lizards on our fences and patio. Where did they go during the winter?

If they can survive birds or cats or other predators, fence lizards in the wild have a lifespan of about four years.

So what do they /do/ during those three or four winters?

They brumate.

Brumation is a lizard's version of hibernation. Hibernation is a bit more complicated in that it involves regulating body temperature and so in. Brumation is just sort of a slowing down of the metabolic processes.

So, fence lizards find some nice cozy spot in your storage shed or under some fallen leaves and sort of sleep for the winter, although they may get up on a warm day to catch some rays and find some food.

For the sake of my dear wife can you explain why older men have runaway eyebrows and what to do about them? The end of one of mine sticks out like Andy Rooney's on "60 Minutes" even though I have my hair person trim the stupid thing every time I get a haircut.

I think bushy eyebrows make older guys look sort of demented, which isn't necessarily a bad thing. In fact, I sometimes try to fluff mine up a bit, depending on the occasion.

Anyway this has to do with something called dihydrotestosterone or DHT, which is something produced in hair follicles out of testosterone. In some cases, DHT causes the hair follicles in guys' scalps to dry up, leading to baldness.

However, for reasons that aren't quite clear DHT also promotes growth of hair on the face and chest. This is why some guys go bald but still have hairy chests and bushy beards. And bushy eyebrows.

Battle of the sexes heats up: To sweat or not to sweat

March 20, 2009

When my husband and I work out, I have the fan blowing on me and he prefers just to sweat a lot. I believe that calorie for calorie I'm still losing as much weight, but I prefer the fan cooling me. while I work. He believes that because it appears that he is sweating more than me, that he is losing more. What do you think?

I think your husband is misguided. Actually, I think he's a dope but "misguided" sounded more polite.

If your husband is sweating, it merely means his body is throwing off moisture that will evaporate on the skin and cool him off. Any weight he might lose by sweating is merely water weight, which he will replenish later.

Meanwhile, you are keeping cool by letting the air flow from the fan speed that evaporation process.

Now, it is entirely possible that your husband really is burning more calories than you, depending on the exercises he is doing and other factors such as speed or duration or weight or stuff like that.

However, just the fact he's all sweaty and you're not, doesn't mean he is burning more calories than you.

What is the origin of the "nick" in "nickname"?

This goes back to the 1300s when the word was "ekename" and meant "an additional name." The "eke" part came from Old English word eaca, meaning "an increase."

Over time, "an ekename" got sort of mashed together into one word—"nickname."

Does getting a blood transfusion change your DNA?

Most blood transfusions only involve red blood cells and such cells do not contain DNA. However, if you got a bone-marrow transplant, you probably would end up with the donor's DNA, at least in your blood.

A full moon ups temperatures, but no one knows why

March 29, 2009

I know that the moon has an impact on ocean tides. I also know that ocean currents have an effect on weather patterns. My question is this: Does the moon have a direct impact on daily temperatures and weather patterns? For example, is it typically hotter on days that have full moons?

It's a good thing I bestirred myself to actually do some research on this one instead of following my first instinct, which was to say this is a silly question and you are a silly person for asking it.

It turns out the moon can have a direct influence on our weather.

One thing I read said daily temperatures around the world rise by about 0.5 degrees during a full moon.

I don't think scientists know for sure why this is so. It could just be the added light hitting Earth's surface warms us slightly, but there seem to be some doubts about this.

One idea is that the Earth is slightly closer to the sun during a full moon so we get a touch more solar radiation.

Another idea is that the moon's gravitational pull creates tides in the atmosphere the same way it creates tides in the oceans.

This would change the temperature at various levels of atmosphere, which would in turn affect the formation of clouds and wind patterns.

All this is a lot more complicated than what you're getting here, but my brain already hurts so I don't care to delve into it any deeper.

Why are there Braille instructions on drive-through ATMs?

Because it is required by federal rules set up by the Americans with Disabilities Act of 1990. Granted, blind people may not be driving themselves up to ATMs—or at least let's hope not—but they do take cabs.

Baseball blasphemy

April 7, 2009

Why does baseball have such a long season? It seems like they could figure out which teams are the best in about one-third the games.

One-third the games? I got a case of the vapors just thinking about it and had to go back to bed for awhile.

Fortunately, I was raised to be tolerant and forgiving of even the most outrageous blasphemies, so I am willing to discuss this in a calm and reasonable manner instead of just screaming at you.

Let us say for the sake of argument we did have a 54-game season instead of 162 games. What would we do for the rest of the summer? Watch golf? Go down to Chase Field and watch live checkers matches? Spend more time with our families reading good books aloud and playing wholesome board games?

What are you? Some kind of nut?

The thing of it is a season reduced that severely might not necessarily end with the best team being crowned champs.

Baseball is a game of ups and downs, streaks and slumps, good days and bad days. Anything can happen. Ask any Cubs fan. And it is very unusual for one team to dominate its division from Opening Day through the end of the season.

So over 162 games things sort of even themselves out.

Major League Baseball has experimented with the split season, and several minor leagues use it. Basically you have two 81-game seasons with the winners of the first half and the winners of the second going to the playoffs. But MLB has decided to stick with one long season.

In the pitchers' box scores what does "NP" mean?

Even I know that one—number of pitches.

Bees swarming around porch light at night is a puzzler

April 10, 2009

One recent night there was a swarm of bees flying around our porch light. I thought it was bizarre, but I left them alone. Then in the morning I walked outside and they were all lying on the ground. It looked like most of them were dead, but one was still moving a bit. Can you explain this occurrence?

Hmm, that's a puzzler. You people probably will have to bail me out on this one.

Honeybees use up a lot of energy buzzing around all day gathering nectar so they tend to rest up at night and keep each other warm. Even swarming bees out on the hunt for a new hive location tend to hole up at night.

Here's my guess: These bees were somehow evicted from their hive by a predator of some sort or because someone tried to destroy it.

Anyway, they were out and about and because bees use sunlight to navigate they were drawn to your porch light. They don't have particularly good eyes, but they do have three organs called *ocelli* that they use to detect light.

So these bees came to your light and because they are not used to artificial lights the way moths or other bugs might be, they landed on the light bulb and got cooked.

What do think? I couldn't find any other explanation, but that doesn't mean there isn't one.

In areas prone to flooding, hundreds or thousands of sandbags are used to curb the threat. What happens to all these bags of sand when the crisis is over?

Sandbags that are still dry after the flood recedes can be salvaged and reused later.

However, bags that are soaked by the floodwaters probably are contaminated by chemicals, dead animals, raw sewage and all sorts of icky stuff. So they have to be hauled away to the landfill.

Pinpointing Ariz.'s lowest spot; battling witches' broom

April 16, 2009

While a friend and I were discussing elevations, she made the remark that she knew we were at sea level because we are in a valley. I told her that was not true and that Phoenix's elevation is around 1,200 feet. But I wonder: Is there any place in Arizona that is at sea level? If not, what is the lowest elevation in Arizona?

Your friend thinks that we are at sea level because we live in a valley? I wonder what other interesting ideas she has.

Anyway, the lowest spot in Arizona is where the Colorado River crosses the border into Mexico near San Luis. It's just 70 feet above sea level.

I found two or three versions of Yuma's elevation, but it seems to be around 137 feet.

One thing I read said the lowest point in the state is Phantom Ranch at the bottom of the Grand Canyon. This, of course, is not true. The elevation down there is 2,550 feet.

Depending on what part of the Valley you're in, our elevation is around 1,100 feet.

There is something called, I believe, witches'-broom. It attaches to a tree and ultimately kills the tree. We see a number of these in our area of Scottsdale. Is there any remedy for this?

Witches' broom is a fungal disease of trees and other woody plants that causes abnormal, stubby growth around buds that sort of looks like a broom or a bird's nest.

Witches' broom sometimes goes by the name of "stubborn," although I think stubborn might be another kind of tree disease. Stubborn is a pretty interesting name for a disease, although I don't know how it came about.

You can ask at a nursery or garden center, but I don't know that there is a reliable cure for witches' broom other than a pruning saw.

Pickled herring cures all; quaggas are striped mussels

April 20, 2009

A friend of mine recently had some surgery and is expected to be laid up for a while, so I did what you probably would do in the same situation. I took her some pickled herring. I mean, what are friends for, anyway?

Sure, I could have taken her some flowers or something, but flowers would fade in a few days while pickled herring, being pickled and all, stays with you a good long time.

My friend seemed a bit nonplussed by this, but I think she was still a bit stoned from the painkillers, so that's understandable. I explained to her that my godmother ate pickled herring and lived to be 107. Every now and then my godmother would announce that she was going to die, but then someone would bring her some pickled herring and she would decide life was worth living after all.

Anyway, my friend is expected to be out of circulation for a couple of weeks, so I hope she eats the pickled herring and doesn't just give it to the cat. Pickled herring would put her back on her feet in no time. I hope so. She's pretty much the only one around the place who knows how to get anything done.

A quagga is an extinct kind of zebra. So why are these mussels that are invading Arizona's waters called "quagga" mussels?

Because they are striped and sort of look like another invasive pest called zebra mussels. I guess they thought they couldn't call them sort-of-look-like-zebra-mussels.

Quagga is an Afrikaan word that seems to have come from a similar native word.

Quaggas were related to (inappropriate term) and zebras. The last one died in a zoo in Amsterdam in 1883.

I am told quagga mussels are edible but tend to be contaminated from pollutants.

Dead or not, scorpion harbors potential for stinging pain

April 27, 2009

If one were to step on a dead scorpion, would one be stung?

Well, that's a pretty good question. I myself don't keep a lot of dead scorpions or other dead stuff around the house to step on, but the other night I did happen to step on a dog toy, in the night and it hurt a lot.

Anyway, did you know that scorpions, or at least the ancestors of our scorpions, are thought to be among the first creatures that crawled out of the sea to conduct business on land about 450 million years ago?

And did you know that meerkats, those cute, sort of ferrety-looking things from Africa that you see in magazines or on TV nature shows love to eat scorpions?

They bite off the scorpion's poison sac before dining, and most of the recipes I found for scorpions advised doing sort of the same.

I found a recipe for scorpion soup that involves 20 to 30 scorpions cooked alive. It sounded pretty interesting, and I really don't really care much about scorpions one way or another, but I don't think I'd care to cook them alive.

Anyway, in answer to your question, I don't think you should step on a dead scorpion, stinger-side up.

Do you remember the column from last week about the lady whose husband had brought a junky car to the marriage and keeps promising he'll fix it up, but it still just sits there in the backyard?

That drew a big response. I never seem to know what's going to appeal to you people.

Many of you suggested turning it the car into a planter, and there were some other good ideas, too, but here's the one I liked best: She should start restoring it herself. He would be out there working on it himself in a flash.

How light penetrates eyes, and Valley's volcanic rocks

May 4, 2009

In the middle of the night, I use a flashlight to get to the bathroom. While sitting there with my eyes closed I can tell when I have the flashlight on or off. How can the light get through my eyelids?

Don't you know your way around your own house well enough to find your way to the bathroom in the dark? None of my business, I suppose, but I was just wondering.

Anyway, it is possible for a limited amount of light to penetrate your eyelids when your eyes are shut. This is called remnant external light or eyelid transmission.

I'm not sure, but I think this is because your eyelids are fairly thin and contain a lot of small capillaries.

According to "Biological Psychiatry," certain colors of the spectrum can do this transmission thing better than others. Red is especially good at getting through your eyelids. Researchers know this because they are studying light treatment during sleep to modify biological rhythms.

Where did all the volcanic rock in the Phoenix area come from? There doesn't appear to be any volcanic-like mountains in the area, and it is generally believed that all the mountain ranges are from uplift.

If you had been around here from 15 million to 25 million years ago, you would have seen plenty of volcanoes.

The Superstition Mountains are the site of at least three major eruptions, maybe more, all those millions of years ago. The Goldfield Mountains in the East Valley and the Hieroglyphic Mountains to the west are both made of volcanic rock.

Big volcanic eruptions can throw dust and ashes for hundreds of miles, so it is possible to have volcanic rock even if there was never an active volcano right there on the spot.

That noise in the night? Maybe it's a belching poodle

May 11, 2009

We have two small dogs. One is a purebred poodle, and the other is a poodle mix. They are about the same age and weight. They both eat exactly the same food. However, the poodle cuts loose with a burp several times a day. I've had lots of dogs over the past 35 years, but I can't remember any of them belching. Passing gas, yes, but belching, no. Any ideas?

A couple.

The dog might be taking in too much air when it eats. I am told that raising the food and water bowls off the ground will help with this, but I'm not sure why.

Or it could be that as the dog gets older its supplies of the digestive enzymes it uses to break down its food decline. That might cause burping.

Check the dog food you're using to see if it contains such enzymes.

It's probably nothing serious, but you might want to ask your vet about it.

Now, remember the one last week from the guy who hears strange sounds at night that he described as the wails of a shrieking baby?

He wanted to know what it was. I threw out a few half-baked ideas, and asked you people if you had any suggestions.

And as usual, you did not disappoint.

There were a lot of votes for frogs and toads and peacocks. I don't know about that. There are peacocks in my neighborhood, and I don't think they sound like a shrieking baby.

Other suggestions: a barn owl, distressed rabbits, coyote pups, a nighthawk, a cockatiel, elk, screech owl, female fox, great horned owl and La Lorna.

La Lorna is a ghost woman who drowned her children and now wanders around at night wailing.

I guess that settles that.

Blame wolf genes for your dog's circling habit

May 28, 2009

I have noticed that my dog always circles in a clockwise direction before lying down. Is this trait dominant in all dogs? Could it be a Northern Hemisphere phenomenon, and dogs in the Southern Hemisphere circle in a counterclockwise direction?

OK, I'll answer this if you people promise you won't start in on me with that hooey about water draining clockwise north of the Equator and counterclockwise south of the Equator. That's just nonsense, but some of you always want to argue about it.

For starters, you have to remember that your pooch and a wild wolf are about 99 percent identical genetically. I don't know what the other 1 percent is. In the case of my dogs, I think it's the dumb gene.

In the wild, wolves will turn around a few times and sometimes dig down into the dirt a bit to make a smooth and cool bed. And trampling down tall grass would keep their field of vision open just in case something tasty happens to wander by.

However, which way the wolf or dog circles before bedding down has nothing to do with which part of the world it lives in or with the Coriolis effect. That effect is what spins winds clockwise in the Northern Hemisphere and counterclockwise in the Southern Hemisphere. You can read about various Coriolis facts and fictions, including the dog thing, at the "Bad Coriolis" page at www.ems.psu.edu.

I wonder if the direction in which a dog circles has anything to do with whether it is right-pawed or left-pawed.

Maybe a right-pawed dog would naturally go clockwise and a left-pawed dog in the opposite direction.

Since about 80 percent of dogs are right-pawed, that would explain why most of them seem to circle clockwise.

Mean old harris hawks

June 2, 2009

To those of you who only read the column online and not in the real paper: I'm sorry it's been missing the last few days.

No, I wasn't in the hospital again or furloughed again. It was a computer problem. And a problem with me being kind of dumb about such stuff.

Anyway, trust me: You didn't miss much. I should know.

And here's today's column:

Why are there more Harris hawks and why are they not eliminated because they are predators and kill bunnies and little birds? And why don't Harris hawks go after pigeons and leave other birds alone? I think about this while I'm sitting in my back yard watching this massacre.

Really, people, I don't make up these questions. This is a real voice mail that came in the other day. I wish I could say this lady was joking, but she sounded pretty serious. And, while I do tend to get a fair number of voice mails from around the time the bars closed, I think she was sober.

Lady: Listen up. Harris hawks are predators. They eat bunnies and little birds and lizards and ground squirrels and stuff like that. They have done so from time immemorial. For heavens sakes. That's their job. That's what they're supposed to do.

You know, I really worry a lot about some of you people. I just don't know how you're going to get by. We've been over this before. You can't just go around "eliminating" things just because they eat bunnies. Sheesh.

As for the pigeon thing, Harris hawks will frighten those pests way, but unless the pigeon is very young or very old or if the pigeon bars have just closed and the pigeon is in some way impaired, Harris hawks aren't especially good at catching them. For that you need something faster, like a falcon.

OK, remember the one that other day from the woman who wondered why her bras have little bows between the cups?

I have since heard from several of you who seem to have given a lot more thought to bras than I have, but there's no room here for that just now. We'll discuss it tomorrow.

That darn bra bow: Decorative trifle or busk holdover?

June 3, 2009

OK, the other day a woman asked her husband why there is a little bow between the cups of her bras and he suggested, apparently being wildly optimistic, that she ask me.

Which she did.

I speculated that it was merely for decoration, sort of a girl thing. Since then, I have heard from a number of you who seem to have given a lot more thought to this matter than I ever have.

You know, I spent years crawling and clawing my way over the broken careers of colleagues, backstabbing and being obsequious and ingratiating all the way, to get to the lowly, underpaid position I now hold, and it's come to this—writing about ladies' underwear.

Oh well, it pays the bills. Or at least most of them. The others I just toss on the pile on the dining room table and hope they go away of their own accord.

So about those little bows: They seem to be holdovers, but holdovers of just what is under debate.

Some of you think they are left over from primitive bras that were cinched up in the middle with a bow.

Some of you think the bows let the wearer know if the garment in turned inside out, but why one couldn't figure that out by ones' self, I don't know. I don't believe I've ever seen a woman wearing a bra inside out, but then I don't generally go around looking at all that many ladies in their undies.

Last but not least, and the idea I tend to believe, is the busk bow theory.

Back in the days when women wore corsets a lot, there was a piece of whalebone or whatever called a busk that was inserted in a sheath down the front of the corset and tied in place with a bow.

The busk is gone, but the bow remains.

"Whiskey tango": It's not a drink, definitely not a dance

June 11, 2009

After your column the other day about dogs drinking beer there was a reader's comment on your website that said there is nothing more "whiskey tango" than getting your dog drunk or giving it "people food." What does "whiskey tango" mean?

Good question. I wondered about that, too, but I was too lazy to look up the answer until you asked.

"Whiskey tango" comes from the military phonetic alphabet for the letters "W" and "T."

It is an email acronym for "(inappropriate term)."

You can learn about all sorts of email/text messaging acronyms at http://acronyms.thefreedict…

My wife and I recently were watching a TV trivia show. The answer to one question had to do with Guam, which I said was a territory, and she said it was a nation. I pointed out that Puerto Rico is also a territory, and she said it was also a nation. Who's right?

She's wrong and you are kind of right.

"Nation" means that a country is sovereign and self-ruling and handles all its own affairs, foreign and domestic.

Puerto Rico is a commonwealth. That means, in a nutshell, that it controls its own internal affairs, but the United States controls stuff like commerce and military matters and so on. The Northern Mariana Islands are a commonwealth, too.

"Territories" gets little more complicated. In a nutshell, they are considered to be unincorporated

Territories" gets little more complicated. In a nutshell, they are considered to be unincorporated areas under the more or less direct control of the U.S. Congress can legislate for territories without their consent.

Would you please tell your readers not to wear aftershave or perfume when they go out to eat?

OK.

Yo-de-o-lay-heee-hoo! All about why the Swiss yodel

June 14, 2009

What's the deal with Swiss yodeling? Did they, or do they, yodel and if they do why?

I know a woman who is very well-educated, very intelligent, very accomplished, deeply spiritual, is comfortably well off, has two daughters, some wonderful grandchildren and has a beautiful voice.

In other words, she has just about anything one might want from life, but she told me once she really wished she could yodel.

I don't blame her. That would be kind of cool.

Anyway, the Swiss supposedly developed yodeling to communicate across deep mountain valleys and later incorporated it into their music.

However, forms of yodeling are common in some other musical cultures, including Persian, traditional Gregorian, pygmy and American bluegrass.

Ok, I'm going to be gone for two weeks. No, I'm not sick again. I'm in the pink.

But I have to take another onerous week of unpaid furlough plus a week of a vacation. I don't know how much more blood my masters think they can squeeze from this stone.

Today's range of questions begin with the Baboquivari

July 3, 2009

Where exactly are the Baboquivari Mountains? How did they get their name, and how do you pronounce it?

The Baboquivaris are southwest of Tucson and stretch down toward the border.

The range's name is a Tohono O'Odham phrase meaning "narrow at the waist." If viewed from a certain perspective, they sort of look like an hourglass tipped over on its side.

As near as I can tell, it is pronounced "BAH-bo-kee-VAH-ree," but I am not 100 percent certain about that.

Baboquivari Peak is the highest point in the range at 7,740 feet.

It is sacred to the Tohono O'Odhams, whose traditions hold that I'Itoi, the god who created them, lives in a cave on the mountain and sometimes comes down to give the people commandments or advice.

Once, legend says, some Spanish explorers were digging for silver or gold in the mountain and it opened up and swallowed them. Served them right.

When the weather people compare current rainfall data to the "normal" rainfall, how do they determine "normal" rainfall?

It's not "normal." It's "average."

They determine it the same way they figure out the average temperatures.

It's the averages over the past 30 years and is updated every 10 years.

Why does the water in my toilet bowl rise and fall when it's windy out?

Because the wind blowing across the top of the vent pipe on your roof creates a kind of suction in the pipe, which causes the water to slosh around.

It is known as the Bernoulli Effect.

Heat, not humidity, messes with cars' power windows

July 7, 2009

My car has power windows and this weekend when it was hot they rolled down, but the windows didn't want to roll back up without my help pushing them up. Now the lady in my carpool said her car had the same problems. Is it coincidence? She thought it was the humidity.

I put this matter to my old pal Mark Salem of Salem Boys Auto in Tempe. He knows a lot about cars. He may know a lot about other stuff, too, but I've only ever asked him about automotive matters.

Anyway, it's not humidity; it's the heat.

According to Salem, the heat probably has caused one connection or another in your windows' motor to expand, thus stopping the flow of power.

So I suppose the thing to do is get rid of the car and buy a new one. Not really. That would be silly.

I think the thing to do is have your mechanic check the connections in the motor that drives the windows up and down and make sure they are good and tight.

As a kid, one of my favorite baseball memories was to arrive early for a game in order to watch both teams go through infield and outfield practice as part of their routine. Whatever happened to this? Is being able to catch, field, and throw/Are catching, fielding and throwing/ no longer skills present-day players need to refine or continue to keep sharp?

Extensive pregame fielding practice seems to have gone the way of a game of pepper in Major League Baseball.

I'm not sure why this is, but here's one idea I came across. Think about it: A coach hits three or four balls right at you and you throw to one base or another or hit the cutoff man. Big deal. That is hardly practice for game-situation plays. That sort of stuff is reserved for spring training or the occasional workout.

Honorifics, wigs bring dignity where it's needed

July 17, 2009

Recently, I've spent quite a bit of time recently watching our state Legislature on Channel 123. Yeah, I know, I should get a more interesting life, but with the budget bungling, I try to keep informed. My question: Why is it that all who appear before any of the various committees have to respond to each question from the politicians by saying "Mr. Chairman" and/or "Senator Whozi" before making a statement or answering a question? It's as if these politicians need to be reminded who they are. Seems to me these are superfluous, time-consuming responses.

Thank you for saving me the trouble of saying you have too much time on your hands. Way too much. I'm glad you to recognize your problem. That's the first step toward getting help.

As for the use of all those honorifics and titles and so on, it's just sort of a ritualized courtesy. I suppose it's meant to add a veneer of dignity to the proceedings.

And heaven knows what they'd call each other if those rituals weren't in place.

I understand that our early colonial statesmen probably wore wigs because the British did, but why did the British wear them? Seems pretty silly.

A lot of people will tell you that upper-class people of the 17th and 18th centuries wore powdered wigs because of lice and because people back then didn't bathe or wash their hair very often. That's not so.

Like so many other things that seem pretty silly, it was just a matter of fashion.

Supposedly the trend started when Louis XIV, the "Sun King" who ruled from in the 16th and early 17th centuries, started going bald. I guess he was kind of like Samson with that whole hair-is-power thing.

The fashion flourished until it finally died out around 1800 or so.

Predicting weather based on quail is for the bird (brain)

July 21, 2009

My boyfriend and I have been noticing that the quail in our area are still hatching new broods. His theory is that this means we are in for a cold, wet winter. My theory is that it means we had plenty of moisture the previous winter and/or spring and that created conditions conducive to the plants and bugs that the quail eat, thus they had plenty of nutrients necessary to breed successfully. Who is correct?

I think someone as astute and no doubt attractive as you should get a smarter boyfriend.

I'd offer to help out in that regard, but I don't really know you, and there are a lot of people out there, including many women, who would tell you I wouldn't necessarily qualify as a smarter boyfriend than the dope you are seeing now. Maybe even a step down.

Still, keep me in mind.

Yes, it is true that some varieties of quail will raise more than one brood per season, but let's think for a minute, shall we?

If the number of quail hanging around was a reliable prediction of what next winter's weather would be like, the National Weather Service wouldn't need all that fancy equipment or highly educated experts, would it? It They could just get a bunch of quail and count how many broods they raise and then make their predictions. Replacing staff with quail would save them a lot of money.

Maybe I shouldn't mention that. It might give the thanes of the Dark Tower some ideas.

Anyway, as you noted, the amount of winter rains and the vegetation and other quail food those rains produce determine how big the season's quail crop might be. A good supply of nutrients triggers the release of hormones that determine just how much whoopee the quail feel like making.

Coyotes that attack birds and pets are no big surprise

July 29, 2009

A companion and I walk my dog on the Bridle Path on Central Avenue in Phoenix at about 5 each morning. The other day, we watched in horror as a coyote ran across the street in the 6500 block of North Central Avenue with a duck in its jaws. There was no question that it was a coyote and not a large dog. The yard from which he emerged previously housed ducks, ducklings and chickens. The coyote had killed the majority of the animals. We had seen coyotes previously in the neighborhood during the winter months. I wasn't concerned when I initially spotted them, but now, I am aware that they are preying on pets. I tried contacting Fish and Game, but they provided no support. What can be done to rid our neighborhood of these animals? Can you suggest an agency to contact?

Hello, lady. Knock, knock: Anybody home?

Sorry, that was unnecessarily snarky, wasn't it?

But c'mon. There are coyotes all over the Valley, and if you're just now catching on to the fact that they eat pets, you need to get out and around more.

Game and Fish isn't going to come out on this, unless one of God's dogs is actually threatening humans. Ducks don't count.

Coyotes are pretty good jumpers, so unless you want to string concertina wire or electrified wire along the top of your fence, you need to keep your small pets inside as much as possible, or at least don't leave them outside unsupervised.

If a coyote does drop by, honk an air horn at it, throw a can full of pebbles or pennies at it, or spray it with a hose.

And if you see one that scored a duck or whatever, well, that's just the way it goes.

Hot food and drinks better than cold for summer

August 6, 2009

Settle this debate for me: Our friends say hot soup, hot coffee and hot foods are good for you in the summer. I say that cold foods, light meals and cool drinks are much better. I've also read that hot foods and high temperatures increase your blood pressure.

There's nothing like a nice big slice of watermelon or a bowl of ice cream on a hot day.

However, your friends are mostly right about this. Don't you feel lucky to have such smart friends?

They are "mostly" right because I think spicy would be a better adjective here than hot, although hot isn't inaccurate.

Think about it for a minute: Why do you think people who live in hot climates tend to eat a lot of hot, spicy foods? Think Indian or Thai or Mexican cuisine.

Have you ever had Jamaican jerk sauce? Unless the cook wimps out, it will just about take the top of your head off.

I don't know about the blood-pressure thing, but eating hot and spicy foods increases your blood circulation and makes you sweat. And sweating, of course, cools you off.

So, a nice hot bowl of soup or some kaeng khiao wan nuea might be just the thing on a hot day.

As long as we're on the subject, do you know why it is that when you eat spicy food no amount of ice water seems to cool off your mouth?

Because spicy foods tend to contain a lot of oil, and that oil sticks to your mouth and tongue. And, of course, oil and water don't mix.

You'd be better off drinking a glass of milk or slowly chewing a plain tortilla. And, of course, there's always good old beer.

Aren't you going to ask me what kaeng khiao wan nuea is?

It's a spicy Thai beef curry.

A bug-eating lizard or sewer roaches—it's your choice

August 12, 2009

Would spreading dog poop along a block wall bordering a wash deter snakes? And are there any repellants I could use to keep lizards away from my water meter box?

Let's talk about the second one first, shall we?

Unless they are the Double Secret Deadly Balinese Instant Death Lizards, what do you care if there are lizards in your water meter box?

(I know I shouldn't have to say so, but there really isn't such a thing as the Double Secret Deadly Balinese Instant Death Lizard. I never quite know about you people, so I thought I should just make that clear.)

Anyway, why are these lizards there?

Because there are bugs and other stuff to eat there, especially sewer roaches. Which would you rather have hanging around—a bug-eating lizard or sewer roaches?

Just leave them be.

Next, about the snakes:

Yes, some snakes, including rattlesnakes, can climb into tree branches and up walls, but whether they can crawl right up a block fence, I don't know. I don't think so, but you never know.

In any event, I doubt that snakes much care one way or another about dog poop. And wouldn't you feel a bit silly putting dog poop along your fence?

I came across some commercial snake repellants that maybe you could find at a big hardware store or a nursery or on the Web, but I can't say if they really work.

I also found suggestions involving diatomaceous earth and cinnamon, but I can't vouch for any of them.

Better yet, you should trim back any tall grass or any tree limbs that might hang over the back of your fence that might give a snake a leg up, so to speak.

Rubber snakes, cutting grass may keep quail away

August 20, 2009

Do you know of anything that I could put under my bushes to stop the quail from laying their eggs? I love the little ones, but with three big dogs and an enclosed yard, it's not fun for me or the poor little ones when the eggs hatch and the dogs think they are tasty treats. I was thinking mothballs, but I am afraid the dogs will eat the mothballs and get sick.

Well, that's a new one. I don't get that many anti-quail questions. They are just so darn cute. Like me. However, I applaud your concern for the chicks.

You could just get rid of the dogs, although I know you wouldn't want to do that. That does cross my mind almost every day around 3 a.m. when my two dogs decide they really, really want to go out to the backyard right now and they'd really, really like it if I went with them. But I keep them anyway.

About deterring quail: We're going to ask your fellow readers for better advice, but I do have a couple of ideas.

First of all, mothballs contain stuff such as naphthalene and something called para dichlorobenzene, neither of which is especially good for you or your dogs or the environment in general.

You might get a bunch of those rubber snakes and put them around where you think the quail might nest. It might not fool them for long, but maybe long enough to get you through the nesting season.

I don't know what your landscaping scheme is—mine is trying not to look—but you might try cutting back the lower portions of the bushes and cutting any tall grass around them.

That would leave the areas where quail might nest exposed enough to make them uncomfortable.

Why would watermelon seeds be poisonous?

August 26, 2009

I happened the other day to run into a friend of mine who is recently home from a trip to her native Italy, and I forgot to ask her the most important question you can ask someone who has been on a trip to Italy or anywhere else:

Did you get anything good to eat?

Ah, well. I'll ask her for all the details later. In the meantime, we have this matter to consider:

Are watermelon seeds poisonous to either humans or birds?

For heaven's sake, where did you get that idea?

I even bothered to check this out to see if there was anything to this—the things I don't do for you people—and found out that a lot of people think watermelon seeds are toxic.

This, of course, is nonsense.

Melons and stuff like apples and cucumbers and gourds and so on figured out millions of years ago that if they got nice and ripe somebody or something would come along and eat them, seeds and all.

And then the seeds pass through the diner's digestive system and bloom into a new generation of whatever that plant might be.

So what would be the point of having poisonous seeds?

How many calories are in a gallon of gasoline?

I'm wondering if this is a trick question. Why would you want to know something like this? It hardly works as the answer to an especially tricky crossword clue.

Whatever.

Depending on where you ask there are more or less 3,000 calories in a gallon of gasoline.

I am told that's about the same as 53 Big Macs.

Of course it would be hard to jam that many Big Macs into your fuel tank. But I suppose that wouldn't be a very good idea anyway.

Al Capone starting the BBB is a ridiculous urban myth

August 31, 2009

I have heard that the Better Business Bureau was started by Al Capone as an extortion racket. Is there any truth to this or is it a ridiculous urban myth?

Gee, I'd never heard that one before, but apparently it pops up every now and then.

Alphonse Gabriel Capone was born on Jan. 17, 1899.

The Better Business Bureau was founded in 1912.

So unless Capone was a 13-year-old extortion prodigy he didn't found BBB. The story is, as you said, a ridiculous urban myth.

The organization was started by Samuel Dobbs, a sales manager for Coca-Cola who was disgusted by irresponsible advertisers.

Some stores charge sale tax on The Republic and some don't. When I bought a paper today I wasn't charged the tax. The clerk said stores that are charging the tax are cheating me and getting an illegal profit by doing so.

I asked the experts at the Dark Tower about this. The sale of newspapers is taxable. Some retailers choose to cover the tax with the listed price of the paper while others tack the tax on to the price. It's up to retailers how to handle it.

How do cows get fat when all they eat is grass? Wouldn't that be an effective weight-loss plan for people?

Cows and other ruminants have a pretty complicated digestive system that involves fermentation. In the rumen—one of the stomachs—are millions of bacteria that break down the cellulose in the grass and convert it into sugars the animal can use.

If you ate some grass it's possible you would get a little bit of sugar, but your tummy isn't equipped to break down the cellulose to get the full nutritional benefits. But if you want to give it a try, my lawn could use mowing.

Bring in the FBI on D.C quarters?

September 9, 2009

Like many people, I have begun collecting the 50 state quarters and saving them in a collector's album. Recently, I have come upon a new one—a District of Columbia quarter. Maybe I have a valuable coin in my possession or maybe I should alert the FBI that somebody is producing counterfeit coins? Please let me know.

Late last year the U.S. Mint said it would issue quarters honoring the District of Columbia and the five United States territories: the Commonwealth of Puerto Rico, Guam, American Samoa, United States Virgin Islands and Commonwealth of the Northern Mariana Islands.

The District of Columbia coin came out in late January and the others are following at intervals of two months or so.

Is there any truth to what a guy told me recently that residents over the age of 70 can get an Arizona fishing license for free?

It's called a Pioneer License. To get one you have to be 70 or older and prove that you have lived in Arizona for 25 consecutive years.

Disabled veterans also can get a free license if they have lived here one year and can show proof from the Veteran's Administration of service-connected 100 percent disability.

I have heard that turkey vultures are scarce or even rare in other places. But here in Prescott we have lots of them. Why?

Turkey vultures scarce? Gee, you can't swing a cat in most of Arizona without hitting a turkey vulture.

Turkey vultures are sort of ugly, but they are very interesting birds.

I read they can fly as high as 15,000 feet, but I don't know for sure that's true.

When threatened they play dead or else throw up on whatever is threatening them.

They winter in Mexico.

Cactus as computer protection: pure hooey

September 12, 2009

I have a friend from China who told me it is a good idea to put a cactus by your computer so it will absorb the radiation from your screen and protect you. She says this is because cactuses live on the desert where they are under a lot of radiation. Is there any truth to this?

Why not put a roadrunner by your computer? They live on the desert and probably absorb radiation, too.

This cactus-and-computer thing is a new one to me, but apparently, it is a fairly widespread batch of hooey.

Let's stop and think more than a minute, shall we?

If our computer screens really were giving off life-threatening or other dangerous levels of radiation, don't you think someone would have noticed by now?

In fact, there have been many studies of this, and they all concluded your screen is perfectly safe.

For the sake of argument, however, let's say a cactus really did protect you from radiation flying out your computer screen. Putting the cactus beside your computer wouldn't help much. It's not like it's a radiation magnet. Radiation pretty much spreads out in all directions.

So, if the cactus was going to do you any good, you would have to put it right there between you and screen, and you'd pretty much have to cover up the screen with it.

Wouldn't you feel a little silly doing that?

How long do grapefruit trees typically live before they die of old age?

It depends on a lot of different things, including drought, disease and so forth.

But assuming it is healthy and properly watered, a citrus tree around here will live to be about 30 or 40 years old. In non-desert areas, they can live about 50 years.

Today, we take up our walking sticks and go outdoors

September 19, 2009

OK, campers, today we're going to put on our big, floppy hats, hiking boots and slather ourselves with sun screen and pack up the cell phone and the GPS and the Swiss Army knife and signaling mirror and a first-aid kit and a rain poncho and extra socks and plenty of water and a big lunch and head off down the trail to the backyard and enjoy the great outdoors.

I've heard or read that if you are hiking with a walking stick and happen to meet a rattlesnake that you should put the stick between you and the snake. What purpose does this serve?

This might surprise some of you, but I am not 100 percent sure about this. I looked around and asked about this matter, and the consensus seems to be that putting the stick between you and the snake will give it something else to think about, other than biting you, to the degree that snakes think about anything much at all.

However, the key thing here is to do it slowly. I mean, if the snake is there coiled and ready to strike, you don't want to make a lot of sudden, quick movements. Put the stick in front of you and stand still and then back away slowly and head back to your backyard like a sensible person.

What is the difference between a raven and a crow?

Crows and ravens are from the same genus—Corvus. (I'm pretty sure I learned what genus means in high school, but it escapes me just now.)

Ravens are bigger and shinier and tend to be better at soaring on updrafts than crows. And crows do that "caw" thing and a lot of other vocalizations while ravens tend to just say "gronk" or something like that.

Some of my masters, plus some other people I know, can just say "gronk," but I suppose that is neither here nor there.

To keep mosquitoes at bay, never let 'em see you sweat

September 23, 2009

I was bitten by a mosquito a few days ago. Yesterday I was bit by another mosquito and earlier today another a mosquito latched on my arm. It seems like every time I get bit by a mosquito, I have several of them hovering around me for several days. My question is: Do mosquito bites attract other mosquitoes?

You mean like lots of sharks being attracted by blood in the water? Nope, it doesn't work that way. It's just that mosquitoes like to bite some people more than others.

There are all sorts of things that make you attractive to mosquitoes. Are you a good listener? A good dancer? Are you well-groomed, financially self-sufficient, and do you have a good sense of humor? Do you....

Oops, wrong list. No, it's not that sort of stuff at all.

Do you wear perfume or cologne and something else sort of smelly? Mosquitoes love that sort of stuff.

Do you sweat a lot? Mosquitoes like 'em sweaty. If you are out jogging and your more prudent mate is home taking a nap. You are more likely to get bitten than the napper because you are sweating and throwing off a lot of carbon dioxide. Movement and CO_2 draws in mosquitoes. Pregnant women give off more carbon dioxide than other women so they tend to get bitten more often.

Actually, researchers say that about 85 percent of what makes you look tasty to a mosquito is determined by genetics. That includes the amount of steroids or cholesterol on your skin or how much uric acid you churn out.

And mosquitoes can sense all this stuff from up to 100 feet away.

So it isn't that one mosquito biting you sets off some sort of feeding frenzy. They just like you.

Half-way note:

Well, you're half way through this book. What do you think? I hope you're having fun. And besides, if you're halfway through it the book probably has coffee stains all over it or a broken spine or whatever so you can't take it back for a refund, so you're stuck with it.

You should have thought of that ahead of time.

Actually, I hope you're not reading all of this all at once. It might be better to dip in and out of it from time to time. That way it won't sort of overcome you. Know what I mean?

"Starboard' term was born in the days before the rudder

September 26, 2009

I've always assumed that the left side of a ship was called the "port" side because ships traditionally docked with that side of the ship next to the pier. But why "starboard" for the right side?

You're right about the port thing. I didn't know that before.

And the reason the port thing came to be has to do with how the starboard thing came to be.

Starboard, of course, means the right side of a ship looking forward from the stern. It is a pretty old word that goes all the way back to the Old Norse words styra, meaning "having a hand in," and bord—"board."

Long, long ago before the rudder came along, ships were steered by a special steering oar at the ship's stern. Since there are more right-handed people than left-handed, this steering oar was located on the right side of the ship.

In Old English, this was steorbord—"the side on which the ship is steered."

So the term transformed from Old Norse to Old English to the modern "starboard."

Now about "port." Since the steering oar was on the right side, the ship would be moored on the left side—the larboard or loading side—to keep from crushing the steering oar. Since larboard and starboard sounded too much alike, the left side came to be called port.

Why are they called "bread-and-butter pickles"?

Bread-and-butter pickles are made in a vinegar-sugar brine seasoned with turmeric, mustard and onions.

I read a few different versions of where the name came from, but the name most likely refers to the fact that bread and butter, and these pickles, make a simple, tasty meal for a field hand or somebody like that.

Harmless snake in your garage of probable hunting

October 10, 2009

People, people, people.

No, I don't know why the paint on the Golden Gate Bridge in San Francisco seems to you to be orange.

No, I can't help you get into solitary confinement if and when you are sentenced to prison later this month.

No, I don't know what that bug that you saw was. You have to be more specific.

I'm not even sure I know the answer to today's question, but I'll give it a shot.

Recently when I let my cat into the garage, it came back in with a 17-inch garter snake dangling from its mouth. I then had to chase the snake around the house. Obviously, I don't leave the door open anymore. I can understand how small snakes can find their way into the garage, but do you know of any deterrent to keep snakes out?

First of all, are you sure it was a garter snake? I mean, it may well have been such a thing, but whatever it was it sounds like it was harmless. Yes, snakes can be kind of creepy, but maybe you didn't have to chase it around your house. It probably would have eventually got bored and left on its own accord.

I don't know just how boring it is around your house, but I suspect it doesn't take much to get a snake bored. Possibly even less than it takes to bore me.

So anyway, about the snake. Why was it in your garage to begin with? Probably because it found some cockroaches or maybe even a mouse that it could eat and that you wouldn't really miss

You can find snake deterrents at your nursery or irksome giant hardware store, but I am not sure how well they work. Or you can just leave the job up to the cat.

You might try trimming the grass around your garage or covering up any openings with hardware cloth.

Hummingbirds don't call Jenny Craig, Weight Watchers

October 14, 2009

Do hummingbirds ever get fat?

No.

On other matters, I heard an interview on the radio this week with the immortal Ernie Banks of the Chicago Cubs. He said one of his aspirations was to win a Nobel Prize. I'm in for that. Mr. Banks, if there is anything I can do, let me know.

I note that a high-end clothing store, Barneys New York, is opening here. When I was a kid in St. Louis there was a very low-end Barney's clothing store. Any connection?

Nope.

I'm dieting and I keep close track of my weight, but I notice that after I take a shower I gain about a half a pound every time. My question is: Does the body absorb that much water during a shower?

It's possible. One thing I read said you could soak up as much as 3 pounds during a long soak in the tub, but I kind of doubt that.

Sometime awhile ago, you told me a large rabbit I saw in Paradise Valley was a jackrabbit. Well, I saw one of them again and this time I noticed the tail. It was at least a foot long and black in color. This was definitely a rabbit, although it sure did not look normal with the long tail. Am I seeing things or is this the way jackrabbits look?

Jackrabbits are not rabbits; they are a kind of hare. And I would be surprised, although not amazed, if you saw one with a foot-long tail. Most of them have a tail of 4 inches or so. Are you sure what you saw was a jackrabbit?

As you know, the water here in the Valley is so hard that I get a lot of chemical buildup on my hummingbird feeders. I was wondering if I could use distilled water to make the feeder food and not cause any harm to the birds?

I wouldn't worry about it if I were you.

Journey into the murky world of raccoon removal

October 17, 2009

I was sitting in a sleazy dive in Shanghai when the man I was supposed to meet came in. He had a patch on one eye, a dirty sailors cap on his head and a long scar on his left cheek.

He recognized our prearranged signal—I was wearing big clown shoes—and sidled over to sit on the bar stool next to me. He stared at his ugly reflection in the mirror for a while and then muttered out of the side of his mouth.

"Raccoons."

"You buying or selling?"

"I just want to get rid of them. They crawl around in my pecan tree and make my dogs bark in the middle of the night."

"It'll cost you. Two dollars Sundays. The rest of the week, 75 cents."

He grumbled, but paid up.

This is what I told him: Soak a bunch or rolled-up towels in ammonia, put them in plastic bags and leave them around the area the raccoons frequent. You need to put them in bags or something because ammonia isn't always so good for plants.

Or you could try dried coyote urine. Where can you get dried coyote urine? That's going to cost you another $2.

This one sounds kind of mean, even for raccoons, but I am told it works: whip up a batch of Rice Krispies treats laced with peanut butter and hot chili peppers and leave them around your yard.

There are some wildlife-removal services listed in the Yellow Pages, but be sure they are properly licensed. Raccoons are a protected species in Arizona, and you need a permit from the state Game and Fish Department to trap or kill one. Even if you are going to live-trap them, you should check with Game and Fish first.

The man with the scarred face grunted and went back to nursing his sloe gin fizz. I walked out into the swirling fog, up $2.

Forest service guy probably right in pine-tree argument

October 20, 2009

The pine trees on our property 20 miles northeast of Show Low are dying. They have big sap clumps on trunks and limbs. The neighbors say it is bark beetles, but I called the Forest Service, and the official there said it is sap moths. In Utah, the trees dying of bark beetles die from the top down, which seems different from our pines. Who is right, my neighbor or the Forest Service guy? More importantly, can we do anything to save our pines? We'd appreciate your help as we are slightly confused and probably too lazy to do further research ourselves.

You're confused and lazy and you're asking me for help? Lady, I invented confused and lazy.

Anyway, did you know that sap beetles are related to the pleasing-fungus beetle? Pleasing-fungus beetle. Is that a great name for a bug or what?

I'm guessing the Forest Service guy was right. I mean, he's with the Forest Service. He ought to know.

So, what you have is sap beetles or maybe pine beetles. They're a lot alike.

Pine beetles bore into the bark of a tree to mate and lay their eggs. The adults die after this, but their offspring spend about a year inside the tree, chewing things up before emerging as adults.

A tree's main defense against such things is to ooze sap or pitch out of the bore holes in hopes of washing out the invaders. Sometimes that works and sometimes it doesn't. That's why you are seeing globs of sap on the tree trunks.

The beetles also bring with them something called the blue-stain fungus. This isn't good for the tree, either.

As for controlling them, there are pesticides you can apply to healthy trees, but once the beetles get a grip, the tree is pretty much doomed.

No luck with Janet Reno? Did you try Henry Kissinger?

October 31, 2009

Why no sale of alcohol before 10 a.m. on Sundays? I wrote to Janet Reno about it and all she said was thanks for writing.

Dude, I hate to tell you this but Janet Reno hasn't been the U.S. attorney general for about a decade or so now. And even if she was still on the job, she wouldn't have anything to do with Arizona's liquor laws.

Your question makes me wonder: Why would you need to buy alcohol before 10 a.m. on a Sunday? Maybe for a tailgate party or a barbecue or something like that? If so, why couldn't you plan ahead a little better or just wait until after 10 a.m.?

The 10 a.m. Sunday thing is just a form of blue laws, which have been around ever since the Puritans came to the New World in the 17th century. They are meant to control behavior on Sundays. I guess the idea is that if you can't drink, you'll go to church. Arizona is one of 15 states with some kind or another of rules controlling Sunday liquor sales.

No one seems to know for sure why are called blue laws. Some people think it's because the Puritans printed the rules on blue paper or bound them in blue covers, but that apparently isn't so.

My husband and I recently attended our first funeral here in the Valley since moving here from Ohio four years ago. During the funeral procession, we noticed almost all cars traveling in the opposite direction on the two-lane road pulled over and stopped. We had never seen this before. Is this a Southwestern tradition?

I don't think it is a particularly Southwestern thing. In fact, I seem to remember getting a question a few years ago from a new-comer who wanted to know why drivers here didn't pull over for funerals.

It's just something some people do to be polite.

EEE-ther oe EYE-ther?

November 7, 2009

How do you pronounce "either?" Is it "ee-ther" or "eye-ther?" I say it's the long "e" sound, but my girl friend and a lot of other people say "eye-ther.

"Sir, you are correct.

All God-fearing, right-thinking, neatly groomed, well-educated, patriotic, warm-hearted, caring people who seem to be instinctively trusted by children and small animals pronounce it "ee-ther."

Only disturbed, Proust-reading, pet-hating, line-jumping, poorly manicured, one-world-government advocates with bad haircuts say "eye-ther."

I'm surprised you had to ask. I thought everybody knew that.

Let's move on to a topic that might not be as widely understood.

I have a dwarf orange tree that finally has produced more than two oranges. In the previous years of two or three oranges, I found something had burrowed a couple of holes in them. and so I have to throw them away. I thought it was a bird, but locals tell me it is likely a pack rat. Any idea of what this is before my crop of 10 is decimated by holes?

Locals tell you? You're not from around here? Do you say "ee-ther" or "eye-ther"? It might make a difference in how I answer your question.

Not really. I'm broad-minded that way.

If it was a rat of some sort—pack or roof—it would have chewed a good-sized hole in your fruit. I learned that a few years ago when I got a similar question wrong.

It's one kind of bird or another soaking up the juice or pulp and leaving an entrance for bugs of various sorts.

Try hanging some aluminum pie pans or strips of reflective tape on the tree.

Pans or tape—EE-ther of them will do.

If you see holiday ads for a traditional dinner, chill out

November 15, 2009

I was looking through the grocery-store ads recently and noticed that some of them don't use the word "Thanksgiving" but talk instead of "traditional dinners." Has Thanksgiving become politically incorrect just like Christmas?

News to me, but I guess I wouldn't be especially surprised to find out if it was so.

True, Thanksgiving does have a certain element of religion to it. I mean, who do you think you're supposed to be giving thanks to? The Easter Bunny?

So, it's possible some non-believers would object, and I bet there will be more people watching football games on Thanksgiving Day than there will be going to church.

And I know that many Native Americans see it not as day of thanksgiving but as a remembrance of Europeans' brutal conquest of their ancestors.

I know a lot of people use the generic "Happy Holidays" around this time of year, but I think that is not so much a PC thing as it is a sort of shorthand to cover the season from now until New Year's Day.

I wouldn't worry about it too much if I were you. You're certainly free to celebrate Thanksgiving however you see fit. If other people don't like it, so be it, but no one is going to tell you how to celebrate.

Except for me: None of those little marshmallows on the sweet potatoes, OK?

A couple of years ago, I bought a Santa Claus melon in St. Johns. The clerk didn't know what it was or how much to charge me. It was excellent. Any idea what this is?

Umm…well, yeah, I know what it is. It's just what you said it was—a Santa Claus melon, also known as a Christmas melon. They are so named because their peak season is December.

Jerk honking behind you lacks good left-turn etiquette

November 22, 2009

The other day I was driving my daughter to school and got honked at to turn left on a yellow light. Of course, I didn't want to turn into oncoming traffic but to turn when it was clear. The driver behind me also turned left with me. The next day I saw the same thing happen to two other drivers. The driver who honked sped away to make up for lost time. Who was in the right?

You know, if I'm daydreaming at a light and don't immediately notice it has turned green, I don't mind if the driver behind me gives a gentle toot. However, I do mind—in fact, hate it—when the moron behind me honks to encourage me to turn by cutting it close with oncoming traffic.

I mean, where do you have to get to that is so important that you have to risk life and limb to get there? Especially if you're a moron. It's not like you're running late for your meeting of rocket scientists.

Anyway, I wonder if this is from a newcomer who is not familiar with Valley drivers' peccadilloes. I used "peccadilloes" only to be polite. What I meant to say is that many of them are jerks.

Assuming you did everything properly and entered the intersection before the light turned yellow to wait for oncoming traffic to pass, you were right and the honker was a jerk. And a moron.

My new aluminum steamer has black stains on it. How do I get rid of it?

I think it's aluminum oxide and that won't hurt you. It might even help protect the aluminum.

If you want to get rid of it, mix 1 or 2 teaspoons of cream of tartar per quart of water or 2 tablespoons of vinegar per quart of water and boil it in the pot for about 10 minutes.

Who knows? Maybe you'll see a Neanderthal in the afterlife

November 24, 2009

Are there cavemen in heaven? I mean, during the course of evolution, when did they become "human beings" with "souls"?

There is some evidence that some early humans, such as the Neanderthals, had some concept of an afterlife. Their dead often were buried with tools and food and sometimes flowers.

What sort of an afterlife they looked forward to, I don't know. You'd have to ask a Neanderthal.

Beyond that, there is no way I'm getting into this. What? Do you think I'm nuts? I'd never hear the end of it.

I'm sure there are hundreds of opinions about this, but I think what it is going to come down to is that you're just going to have to wait and find out for yourself.

I have a friend who works as a waitress. She says that when all the snowbirds start coming back, the Canadians typically tip less than everyone else. Is this a cultural thing or do servers in Canada make a better hourly wage and therefore don't rely as much on tips as part of their income?

One of my daughters worked off and on as a "waitperson." On the rare occasions I get to dine out with her, she always takes my wallet and announces that she will determine the tip.

Now, I am by no means a cheap tipper, but it turns out that when she leaves the tip—with my money—I am a remarkably generous, perhaps even extravagant, tipper.

I looked into this matter quite a bit and found no evidence that Canadians tip any more or any less than people in the states do.

I suppose it is possible that winter visitors from Canada or from anywhere else might be on a tight budget and so might not be inclined to be lavish tippers. What do you people think?

How "cran' got linked with the berries

November 28, 2009

Today, we have a few assorted food questions, although this is being written on the day after Thanksgiving, so the topic holds little interest for me. I really don't think I'm ever going to eat again.

Anyway, did you know that a "cran" is a package of 1,200 herrings? Nobody seems to know where that came from. It's a lot herrings, though.

But that doesn't have anything to do with cranberries.

The "cran" in cranberries is a bit hazy. It's probably an American adaption of the Low German word "kraan," meaning "crane," like the bird.

There are different ideas how the berries came to be named for cranes. Some people think it was because cranes liked to eat them. Some say it's because the plant in some stages of development resembles the neck, head and bill of a crane.

In England, the Old World version of the cranberry is called marshwhort or fenberries. "Fenberries" doesn't sound so bad, but I don't much like the sound of "marshwhort." The Algonquian name for the plant is *popokwa.*

Does toast have more or fewer calories than plain bread?

Neither. Toasted and untoasted bread have pretty much the same number of calories. Why wouldn't they?

We have an old family recipe for eggnog that includes two dozen raw eggs and a liter of bourbon. Would the alcohol kill any bacteria, such as salmonella, in the eggs?

Maybe, but only if you leave it in the refrigerator for several weeks before serving,

Green pecans felled by storm can be set aside to dry

December 9, 2009

Monday's storm knocked a bunch of pecans off my tree and a great deal of them are still in the green shell. Are they still good? If they are still good, can I remove the green shells or should I leave them on until they change color? Or will they even do that?

I do not know much about pecan cultivation. When my daughters were younger and we'd be driving to Tucson, I always told them when we drove by those pecan groves along the interstate that we'd better hope never to break down or have a flat tire there at night. Night is when the Pecan People come out and carry their victims deep into the groves and enchant them so they grow limbs and leaves and turn into pecan trees.

I don't think they believed me. They're pretty smart.

I am told that you should if your windfall pecans are looking kind of green, the best thing to do is to put them aside in a dry, well-ventilated area so that the kernels will dry. On green pecans this normally takes about a week to 10 days. After this, crack a few and see if they easily separate from the shell. If they do come away from the shell OK, the kernels still need to be left out to dry for a day or so or they'll go all moldy.

The other day I went out to get my paper at 6 a.m. and checked the bird bath water and it was fluid. I checked it again at 7:30 a.m. and it was frozen. What's up with that?

This one is becoming sort of a winter perennial.

At night the Earth cools off and it keeps cooling off until a bit after the sun comes up. However, sunlight doesn't heat the air it passes through. It heats the sidewalks and your coat and the roof of your car and so on and that heat is radiated into the air around it. So the coldest part of the day usually comes just after sunrise.

Waxy blobs on trunk of palo brea give the tree its name

December 22, 2009

Palo verde ("green stick" in Spanish) is sensible for the so-named trees. But how did the palo brea ("tar stick") tree get its common name? I can't see how it has anything to do with tar.

I'd never heard of the palo brea before, but it turned out that wasn't too surprising.

The palo brea is just one of a variety of different kinds of palo verdes.

There is the blue palo verde, the foothills or little leaf palo verde, the Mexican palo verde, a hybrid called the Desert Museum palo verde and the palo brea, also known as the Sonoran palo verde.

One thing that is interesting about the palo brea is that while most of the other varieties are pretty much limited to the Sonoran Desert, the palo brea also grows in Venezuela and Peru. I wonder why.

The palo brea got its name from some waxy little blobs that form on the green bark of its trunk. Native Americans used to gather this waxy stuff, melted it and used it to glue leather and other stuff that needed gluing.

Any idea why tennis players don't wear gloves?

Any of my own ideas? Nope.

However, I did look around a bit and found some ideas. If they are correct or not, I cannot say.

First of all, some players do wear gloves, especially if they live in a climate colder than ours or if they are getting blisters on their hands.

Next, I am told that players feel that gloves will hinder their ability change their grip as might be necessary or to feel the feedback from the racket. I don't know what kind of feedback you get from a tennis racket, but there you have it.

Consider golfers. They wear a glove on the hand they rely on for power and not one on the hand they rely on for control.

Handicapped-parking rules apply to everyone

December 28, 2009

I am a disabled vet who recently stopped at a bank in Sun Lakes and tried to park in a disabled slot. It was taken by a white van with government plates. I asked the passenger why they were parked there and was told that government vehicles are exempt from the disabled-parking law. Is this true?

As near as I can tell, the person you spoke to was a chowderhead or a jerk or maybe both or possibly just a misinformed passenger. Or there is a chance the driver might be exonerated.

The Arizona rules say you can't stop, stand or park in a spot designated for disabled-drivers' parking unless you have the special license plates or one of those placards that hang from the rearview mirror.

However, because I believe in the inherent goodness of people, I should point out there is one exemption that says: "A person who is chauffeuring a person with a physical disability without a placard or international symbol of access special plates may park momentarily in a parking space provided pursuant to this article for the purpose of loading or unloading the person with a physical disability, and a complaint shall not be issued to the driver for the momentary parking."

So maybe the driver was just inside the bank for a few minutes helping a disabled passenger do business. That's a sweetness and light sort of explanation, isn't it?

Or maybe it's just that the driver of the government vehicle was an ignorant, rude chowderhead jerk.

Just where and what are the "cockles" of my heart?

Nobody knows for sure.

There are two or three explanations, but in one way or another they all seem to refer to the Latin phrase for the chambers of your heart: cochleae cordis.

Something's fishy about claim of electricity in eel skin

January 13, 2010

My husband has a wallet made from eel skin. When he was paying for gas, the attendant saw his wallet and wanted to know what it was made from. She then told him if he carried any credit or debit cards in it, the electronic information would be erased because of the electricity in the eel. Is this so? And does the electricity stay in the skin even after it has been removed and processed to be used in products?

You know, someday you people are going to run out of questions that involve hooey and then where will I be? I might have to answer questions that require some actual thinking on my part or, even worse, work.

Fortunately, that's not the case today. The idea that eel skin erases magnetic stripes has been around for quite a while. It was hooey when it surfaced 20 or 30 years ago and it is still hooey today.

The source of this eel-skin idea is that manufacturers of wallets or whatever used to use magnetic clasps. That's what rubbed out the magnetic strips, not the eel remains.

For another thing, eel-skin stuff isn't made from electric eels and even if it was, the eel would be dead. How electric could they be if they're dead?

Eel-skin accessories are either made from commercially raised eels from various Asian countries where they eat a lot of eels or from an eel-like fish called the Pacific hagfish or slime eel.

Why do they call it a slime eel? Trust me, you don't want to know, especially if you're eating breakfast just now.

What is the origin of the phrase "can of corn" to mean an easy fly ball to the outfield?

In the old days most of the goods were behind the counter and a storekeeper would use a stick to knock down stuff, such as a can of corn, from a high shelf and catch it easily.

When it comes down to flatulence, skills don't matter

January 19, 2010

Is it possible to be flatulent in your sleep?

Sigh.

You know. I've worked for newspapers for many years. I've had lot of different beats. I have honed my craft, sharpened my skills.

And it comes down to this—answering fart questions.

Sigh.

Oh well, as long as you asked, yes, people pass gas while they're asleep. It happens all the time. I even found some videos of people doing that, although why anyone would video such a thing is beyond me.

Let's move on to something more enlightening, shall we?

My husband and I are wondering why there is a French entrée called chicken cordon bleu. There is no blue cord involved.

The cordon bleu was a wide blue ribbon once worn by France's highest order of knighthood, L'Ordre des Chevaliers du Satin-Espirit, founded in 1578. So giving that dish that name would, by extension, make it sound classy.

There is some question whether chicken cordon bleu is of French origin.

People who follow such matters say it probably is a fairly new American dish based on various European recipes. It became widely popular in the United States in the 1960s.

We see the weather report showing 0.10 inch of precipitation fell in Flagstaff. What would the equivalent be in snowfall?

It depends. Most people say one inch of rain is the equivalent of 10 inches of snow.

However, it depends on what kind of snow you're talking about.

You'd have to melt 100 inches of dry, powdery snow to get 1 one inch of water.

On the other hand, 3 inches of wet, heavy snow would be the same as 1 inch of rain.

Fish are off the hook during cleanups of Valley canals

January 24, 2010

I'm told the Salt River Project drains canals every winter for maintenance. Jogging down the canal lately, I see the water getting very low. My question: What happens to the fish and ducks in the canal?

The fish, especially the white amurs SRP stocks in its canals to keep down vegetation, are herded to safety.

The ducks presumably fly or maybe waddle away to other canals or ponds or lakes.

The cleanup crews find all sorts of stuff in the dry canals. Lots of shopping carts, of course, and sometimes guns or safes. Once they found a Corvette.

I recently bought a small box of thyme that was labeled "Product of Israel." When I opened it, there was a cute little black-spotted green beetle-type insect. I was going to release it outdoors because I don't like to kill anything, but my husband thought it would unleash a dangerous new pest into urban Arizona. I don't like to kill bugs as a general rule (except scorpions), so I had to leave the yard while he did the dirty business.

First of all, not to be snarky, but scorpions are not insects. They're arachnids like spiders or ticks or mites and a bunch of other stuff.

Next, I'm sorry, but I couldn't find anything that resembled your description of this thing.

Third, I doubt very much if it would have been an invasive species, and I don't like to go around squishing stuff, either. But maybe your husband was wise to err on the side of caution anyway.

What is the difference between trade paperbacks and mass-market paperbacks?

Trade paperbacks tend to be larger and printed on a good quality of paper. Mass-market paperbacks are smaller, printed on cheaper paper and sell for a cheaper price.

Don't squish phone batteries but do smash stray bugs

January 29, 2010

Is it true that if you answer your cell phone while it is plugged into the charger, it will catch on fire?

My first instinct about this one was to dismiss it as further proof of the willingness of so many of you people to believe anything you read on the Internet, including stuff in this column.

However, in the interest of finding snarky things to say about it, I decided I would spend some time looking into the matter and it turns out there is some—some, mind you—truth to this.

It doesn't seem to have anything to do with whether or not the phone is plugged into the charger.

But it seems that if you're using some cheap-o battery, a counterfeit not supplied with the original equipment, or if the battery is somehow damaged, it can catch on fire or maybe even explode.

My favorite account of something like this was from South Korea or someplace like that where a warehouse worker was killed by an exploding cell phone battery and everyone was mystified until a co-worker admitted he had run over the guy with a forklift, crushing the phone.

I guess I shouldn't say that's my "favorite" story about such a tragedy, should I? Still it's a pretty good story.

Anyway, if you have to replace your cellphone's battery, use only the brand it came with and don't slam it to the ground or something like that.

And watch out for forklifts.

If heaven has operas, Rabbi Plotkin will sing in them

February 5, 2010

Did you happen to see in Thursday's paper that Rabbi Albert Plotkin had died? It ran on Page B6.

My masters do not consult me on such matters, but if they had, I would have counseled them to put it at least on B1 if not A1.

Rabbi Plotkin was a short guy, but he was a giant in the Valley ecumenical movement and especially in the Valley civil-rights movement.

Plus, he knew a lot of funny stories.

R.I.P., Rabbi Plotkin. If they have operas in heaven, I'm sure God will want you to sing in one.

On to other matters:

On The Republic's *weather charts there is a key that shows "r" means rain and "sh" means showers. What is the difference between rain and showers?*

In a nutshell, showers are scattered over a limited area. Rain means it is going to rain over a large area. So, if it is raining in Glendale but not Surprise, that would be showers. If it is raining across a wide area of the Valley, that would be rain.

Big monsoon storms can be very spotty, as you know, but I don't think they qualify as showers. The forecasts for these just calls for thunderstorms.

What is the patch that many NFL players wear on their uniforms? It has a big "C" on it and a certain number of stars.

The "C" stands for "captain" and the number of stars show how many years the player has been captain.

This is a fairly new thing, and why the NFL thought it was necessary I don't know. Maybe to let the refs know who to talk to in case of a rules infraction when someone had to decide whether to accept or decline the penalty.

Some teams just have one captain, and some designate captains for the offense, defense and special teams.

No need to pucker up, Meyer lemons are a bit sweeter

February 20, 2010

My friend has a tree that grows fruit that looks like a small orange. They're not those lumpy-bumpy ornamental oranges and they taste like lemons. What gives?

It's hard to tell without actually seeing them, but I'm not about to drive all over town looking for your friend's tree.

However, I am almost 100 percent sure that they are Meyer lemons, a cross between a regular lemon and a mandarin orange.

Most of the stuff I read about this started with "Scientists believe…" In other words, a Meyer lemon is a naturally occurring phenomenon, a hybrid that seems to be several hundred years old.

They are named for Frank Meyer, a "plant explorer" for the U.S. Department of Agriculture who found them growing wild in China. He brought them to the United States in 1908.

Plant explorer—that sounds kind of neat, doesn't it? I wonder if the USDA still uses that as a job title.

Meyer lemons grow pretty much where other citrus grow. They are usually at their peak in January.

I've never had one, but I am told they are less acidic and sweeter than regular lemons and taste a bit like lime, lemon and mandarin mixed together.

They supposedly make good lemonade that doesn't need as much sugar as lemonade made from ordinary lemons.

They make good soufflés, but I couldn't make a soufflé on the best day of my life, so I guess I'll never know about that. And they make a good lemon curd.

I found several recipes using Meyer lemons, including one called lemon pot de crème. I wonder what that is. The picture of it doesn't look too great.

And I found a recipe for lemon and thyme crème brulee. That sounds pretty tasty.

A few theories on why dogs roll around in stinky stuff

February 25, 2010

The day after my husband commented that our yellow lab kept itself very clean, it made a dash across a field to find some very dead raccoon remains to roll around in. Why do dogs enjoy wallowing in such incredible stenches?

My first thought was that it's because dogs are dumb, but then I thought about it and realized that my two dogs, Goofy and Goofier, don't roll around in smelly stuff, and neither does our guest dog, the queen of planet Urine-us. Of course, I don't tend to have all that many dead raccoons around the place.

There are two or three ideas about why dogs like to perfume themselves with reeking stuff.

Some dogs do it just after they've been groomed and bathed with a scented shampoo that might smell good to you but is a stench to the dogs. So it rolls around in stuff to cover up the smell.

Or dogs might do it instinctively to cover up their own smell. So when the ancestors of your miniature poodle were out stalking a mastodon or something, they would mask their scent by rolling around in stinky stuff so the mastodon wouldn't suspect that a pack of miniature wolves was on its trail. They would just think some dead stuff was following them. This might explain why mastodons are extinct.

Or the dog might to do it to mark the dead stuff as its own or to carry a message back to the pack that it had found some really neat dead stuff and they should all come over for dinner.

OK, remember the one the other day about Olympic gold medals being silver-platcd with gold? They are plated with about a quarter ounce of gold, not a quarter inch.

Inches, ounces. Ounces, inches. You people shouldn't be so picky.

Javelina are not rodents, OK? But they taste good in chili.

March 7, 2010

I hope you can settle a dispute I am having with my friends. I enjoy going javelina hunting every February, and yes, I do eat the meat. I have great recipes for javelina burritos and chili. Some of my friends won't try my burritos because they have heard or read somewhere that the javelina is part of the rodent family. I believe that is just an old urban myth, and I think the javelina is instead part of the swine family. Who is right?

Rodents? Where did they get an idea like that? I swear, sometimes I think you people think that any mammal that is not a dog or a cat or a Holstein is a rodent.

Anyway your friends are wrong and so are you, but you're not as wrong as your friends.

Javelinas—more correctly, collared peccaries—and pigs (swine) are members of the order Artiodactyla, suborder Suiformes. They share a common ancestry that goes back about 30 million years.

However, there are some major genetic and anatomical differences between javelinas and swine, so they are placed in different families. Javelinas are members of the Tayassuidae family and swine belong to the Suidae family.

Actually, a couple of javelinas' closest relatives are the hippopotamus and rhinoceros.

Various other tayassuids have turned up in the fossil record for all the continents except Antarctica and Australia, but peccaries evolved only in North America and went on to migrate south through Central America and to as far as Argentina.

Swine are creatures of the Old World, probably Europe.

So, your friends are totally wrong, and just for that, I wouldn't let them have any javelina chili or burritos. It would serve them right for doubting you.

Your curiosity is a common sound, like animal accents

March 12, 2010

Do animals have accents?

You people just never stop wondering about stuff, do you? I'm not complaining, mind you. It just shows how smart you are.

Of course, I suppose if you were really smart, you'd be reading the grown-up columnists and not this nonsense, but I'll take readers when I can. I need the work.

Yes, various animals of the same breeds or species do have regional accents and dialects. In fact, it seems to be quite common.

For instance, studies of frogs in several countries have found distinct dialects or accents among the same species. Why anyone would study frog dialects, I don't know, but there you have it.

I am told that cats in Japan meow differently than cats in Australia, and that urban birds sometimes sing differently than rural birds of the same species, and that dairy cows in England have different styles of mooing than cows of the same breed living down the road.

Why is this so? I don't think anybody knows for sure.

It could be an evolutionary sort of thing—maybe animals of the same breed/species just get used to the sounds of their comrades around them.

Or it could be that humans in different regions hear animal sounds differently than folks in other areas do.

For instance, I am told that in Spain say, "wu, wu" while in France they say, "bow, bow."

That may well be. I don't know, but if one of my dogs started saying "wu, wu" I think I'd take it to the vet. Or maybe give it some cooked rice. That's supposed to be good for dogs with stomach aches.

But then at my house my dogs only have two things to say: "Let's eat," and "Duh."

Any way you slice it, refrigerated onion won't poison you

March 21, 2010

I recently read an article about food poisoning that said that onions, after being cut open, are a huge magnet for bacteria, especially uncooked onions. It also said that you should never keep a portion of a sliced onion, even if it is refrigerated, as they become highly poisonous even after a single night.

I know I've said it before, and I know some of you think it is patronizing, but people, people, people. I worry about you so much.

Where do you get these ideas? In the office break room? During the coffee hour at church? In supermarket tabloids? Or do you just hear it from your little friends out at the playground?

No, a sliced onion left in the refrigerator, is not going to turn toxic overnight. Of course, it helps if you wrap it in plastic wrap so everything else doesn't end up smelling like onions.

And, of course, if you leave a sliced onion—or anything else— in the fridge long enough it will go bad. But not overnight.

People believe a lot of things about onions, and, I suppose, some of them might be true, or at least half true.

Some people believe that if you leave a bowl of sliced onions around, they will suck up the flu virus or other nasty stuff. Some people say that onions are good for a toothache and that onion juice is good for earaches. I can't think of the last time I had an earache, but if I ever do, I'm sure I'm not going to want to pour some onion juice in there.

Maybe, maybe not. It is true that onions have a lot of sulfur. That's why they make your eyes water when you cut them.

But that same sulfur is a pretty good germ killer. So, just leaving a sliced onion wrapped in plastic wrap and kept in the refrigerator is not going to turn poisonous overnight.

Don't mess with grumpy old men if you want to win

March 26, 2010

Perhaps you could settle a bet between my husband and me. We are wondering what age bracket you fall into. My husband says you're a grumpy old man. I say you're just grumpy. Who's right?

The last I checked, the female-male score was 9 or women, 5 for men.

However, I calling this one a no-score. Maybe I'm old and maybe I'm not. None of your business. But I can tell you I don't have a grumpy &#*@& bone in my @%$#*& body. Ask anybody who *#*&(knows me.

So there.

You know, I used to get questions from some of you people asking if I am a male or female. That was pretty funny.

Men have Adam's apples, and women don't. The other day I noticed that my two male cats also have Adam's apples, and I got to wondering if this is true of all animals. Do animal males have them and females don't. If so, why? And what is their purpose?

The consensus seems to be that both men and women have Adam's apples. (It is named for the idea that back there in the Garden of Eden Adam gagged on the forbidden fruit Eve gave him. I find this to be a highly dubious idea.)

The Adam's apple is a hunk of bony cartilage wrapped around the larynx—your voice box.

That bony cartilage is thicker and more prominent in men than in women.

That's what gives manly men their deeper, manly man voices. They are thinner on females which gives them their higher, girly girl voices.

As to whether animals also have Adam's apples, the jury seems to be out.

Some people say yes, and others say no. I'm leaning toward yes.

(Deep sigh): Red tape on poles not for invading army

March 30, 2010

I live near 64th Street and Cactus Road. Red reflective tape is appearing on the aluminum poles of the street signs. There are usually three wide bands of tape placed about a foot apart on each pole. Each week, more poles are being red-taped. My neighbor told me that this is being done as a route for a foreign, non-English speaking military to follow, if they are ever in this country to assist with civil unrest. Is this really why this tape is being put on these poles? I have noticed that the poles in question, if followed, lead to a main thoroughfare.

Umm…a week or so ago I got an e-mail from a reader who said I am mean-spirited and insult readers and am just an all-around jerk. That made me feel kind of bad.

So, let me consider some nice, polite, tactful response to this.

Umm…I can't.

Your neighbor is dumb.

OK, OK, not dumb. Misguided, perhaps.

Umm…no, I'm going to stick with dumb.

Why exactly does he think a foreign, non-English-speaking army, say from Mexico or Canada, would come to 64th Street and Cactus Road to assist with civil unrest?

And don't you think if they were to do so, they would send along a few English speakers or at least somebody who could read street signs?

I mean, what if this foreign, non-English-speaking army wanted to stop at McDonald's for an Egg McMuffin and some coffee or whatever? What are they going to do? Point and grunt?

And, of course, the signs, if followed, lead to major thoroughfares? Aside from "Dead end" or "No outlet," most signs do.

As best I know, the red reflective tape is put on these sign posts to increase their night-time visibility so people can see them more easily.

Only a cheater would use hard-boiled eggs in an egg toss

March 31, 2010

Please let me know if you have any tips on how to win our family's annual egg toss—cheating or otherwise.

You'd cheat at egg tossing? Against your own family? At Easter? Geez.

Maybe you should consider seeking public office. You might go far.

We all know what an egg toss is, right? You line up teams of two with the partners facing each other. Then the teams toss a raw egg back and forth, taking a step back with each successful toss, successful meaning the egg doesn't break. The winners are the team with the longest toss.

According to the World Egg Throwing Federation (really), the world record for egg tossing is 323 feet. I find that kind of hard to believe, but if the World Egg Throwing Federation says it's so, who am I to argue?

Anyway, if you want to win an egg toss by hook or by crook, the obvious answer is to somehow equip your team with a hard-boiled egg. Of course, if you were found out it could lead to some hard feelings on the part of your family. And you might be banned for life by the World Egg Throwing Federation.

Egg tossing seems to be a very popular subject in physics classes because it involves things like momentum and impulse and mass and velocity and maybe some other stuff. I'm not sure.

Here's the deal: Think of a ballplayer catching a fly ball. The momentum of the ball is absorbed by the glove and the fielder keeps moving his or her hands back a bit, which slows down the impact.

So here's what to do with the eggs. Stand partially turned away from your partner and catch the egg by cupping it in your hands and letting your arms swing back.

Or cheat. Whatever.

Blessed with serious questions from the peanut gallery

April 19, 2010

Today is Children's Day here at Valley 101 as we take up a couple questions from our younger friends who, God help us, are our hope for the future.

The first one comes from an undoubtedly cute little girl who claims her name is Ellise. She didn't say how old she is.

I accidentally cut off my dog's whiskers. My dad says they won't grow back. They do grow back, don't they?

This is one of those questions that in and of itself is much more interesting than the answer.

How does someone accidentally cut off a dog's whiskers? Why was a child with scissors even allowed to go near the family pet? How dumb does the dog look without its whiskers?

Oh well, the answer is, don't worry. Your dog's whiskers will grow back and rather quickly at that.

In fact, I am told some groomers routinely cut dogs' whiskers. I don't know why.

Next comes 9-year-old Kamyrn who wants to know:

Why do people say "God bless you" when someone sneezes? It's gross to bless the person who sneezes because of the boogers.

This is kind of interesting.

Most people think the custom goes back to the great epidemics of the Black Death. If someone sneezed, it might mean they were coming down with the plague so the people near them wished for their divine protection.

However, there are all sorts of superstitions about sneezing in many cultures.

In ancient Greece, sneezes were thought to be omens from the gods. In Europe, people used to think that when you sneezed, it might be the Big One, so your buddies asked for the Lord's blessing.

And, in some Asian cultures, it was thought that a sneeze meant someone was talking about you behind your back.

Can roadrunners be harmful to the roof of your home?

April 23, 2010

Will a roadrunner that lives on your roof cause damage? My wife says yes and I say no. The roof is a heavy tile roof and the roadrunner cannot get into the attic.

You have a roadrunner living on your roof? That's kind of cool.

I'm going to side with the men on this one. As long as the bird isn't leaving dead stuff up there or prying up the tiles to make a nest, I think it will be OK. The nesting thing is possible, I suppose, but it seems unlikely for a bird of that size.

So now it's Women, 13; Men, 10.

Remember the one that other day from the little girl whose dad told her their dog's whiskers wouldn't grow back after she cut them off?

Her father was wrong, and some of you said I should have given the females a point for that. However, there wasn't any disagreement involved, so it wasn't eligible for scoring. And besides, it would have been a little kid against her father. Hardly a fair fight.

I was told that I could not put pecan branches or leaves in our garden compost, but my adviser didn't know why. It got me thinking that I've noticed there are hardly ever any weeds growing in a pecan grove. Is there something toxic about pecan foliage?

Your friend was misinformed. Pecan branches and leaves are not toxic and can be composted or used as mulch.

Your friend probably got the idea from the fact the pecan trees are sort of related to black walnut trees and black walnut trees can cause you all sorts of problems.

The roots of black walnuts contain a chemical called juglone that is toxic to any other plants within the root zone.

That keeps the competition down.

Did you ever wonder why snakes can't crawl backward?

June 11, 2010

Can snakes move backward?

Didn't we do this one before? I can't remember. Of course, I can't remember why I just found a package of Brussels sprouts in my freezer. I guess it's because I am partial to Brussels sprouts, although nobody else I know seems to be.

Anyway, about snakes going in reverse:

Have you ever examined a snake's scales? Neither have I, nor do I care to do so. But if we looked at them, we would see the scales overlap backward, away from the head. So going backward wouldn't work.

Think about going to the beach and getting sand in your swim suit while you were trying to boogie board or do something else dumb like that. That would be a tad annoying, yes? The same thing would happen to a snake going against the grain of its scales.

Now, a snake could go backward if you picked it up by its tail and dragged it toward you, although it's hard to imagine under what circumstances you might want to do so.

Sea snakes—shudder—can swim backward, but they have the benefit of buoyancy or whatever.

But since you are pretty much unlikely to come across a sea snake here in Arizona, I'm betting you're not going to meet up with a snake slithering in reverse.

Now, remember the one the other day from the woman who thought a perfect baseball game would be all strikes?

It turned out this happened once.

On May 13, 1952, Ron Necciai threw a perfect game in the Class D Appalachian League, striking out all 27 batters he faced. An arm injury ended his career after he won one game for Pittsburgh.

Who knew?

Some archaic (but interesting) facts about greyhounds

June 19, 2010

Has a racing greyhound ever caught the electronic rabbit?

After all these years, I am slowly grasping the idea that I shouldn't answer questions with an unequivocal yes or no because there always seems to be some obscure exception to the rule.

So, about this one, the answer is I'm pretty sure that never happened—but what the heck, you never know.

Greyhounds have a pretty interesting history, if half of what I've read is true.

Did you know they can hit speeds of up to 45 mph and spot prey from as far as half a mile away?

They are traditionally considered to be the dog of royalty.

In ancient Arabian culture, greyhounds were the only dogs allowed into their master's tent or to ride on his camel. I'd like to see a greyhound riding on a camel. That would be something.

Egyptians had favorite greyhounds mummified and entombed with them.

And they are the only dogs identified by name in the King James Bible—Proverbs 30: 29-31, although later translations seem to drop the reference.

In medieval Europe, owning a greyhound could get you executed unless you were of noble blood, and when the ordinary folks were allowed to own them, the dog's toes were broken so it couldn't be raced. I wonder if that's true. It sounds a bit harsh, doesn't it?

Have you ever considered adopting a retired greyhound racer? I would if I didn't already have Dumb and Dumber. They're enough for me.

I used to baby-sit a greyhound. It was a really sweet creature, but like most predators that rely on short bursts of speed, it slept a lot. It was like baby-sitting a potted fern.

Newbie has a lot to learn about Ariz. snakes, scorpions

June 23, 2010

I am new to Phoenix so this may have been addressed previously. I have found small scorpions and snakes in my yard. I thought they were giant earthworms and my cats like to catch the snakes and bring them in the house. Are either snakes or scorpions dangerous to the cats?

Giant earthworms? Gee, you are new to these parts, aren't you?

I'm thinking that if your cats haven't rolled over and died with their little cat feet sticking up in the air after capturing these snakes and bringing them into your house to show you what deadly killers they are, they are not catching venomous snakes.

However, since you are a newcomer, I would suggest that you Google "Arizona venomous snakes" to see some pictures of what dangers might be lurking out there for little Socks and Fluffy.

I'm sure most of the cats' prizes are harmless, but you never know when one of them might tangle with a deadly Giant Argentine Cow-Killing snake. If there were such a thing.

Now, I have a question. Why are you letting Snowball and Tinkerbell roam around killing stuff, anyway?

They are not natural additions to the system around here. Keep them inside.

About scorpions: The kind you need to worry about are bark scorpions, the ones that can climb vertical surfaces, like up your bathroom wall until they nestle into your towel and wait for you to get out of the shower and dry yourself and then they sting you in the butt. I know somebody who had such an experience.

There is some thought that cats are immune to scorpion stings, but no one seems to know for sure if that's true.

And chickens. Chickens are said to be hell on scorpions.

Allegation of vacuousness leaves me feeling empty

June 25, 2010

I got a note the other day from a gentleman who said I am vacuous.

I was pretty sure I knew what vacuous means, but I looked it up anyway. It's not a compliment. I don't believe anyone had said before that I am vacuous, although I have been called a number of other things.

The gentleman did not cite any particular column that led him to conclude that I am vacuous. I guess he just finds me vacuous in general, sort of all-purpose vacuous.

Well, as long as I am vacuous, I might as well cook up a vacuous answer to today's question.

We are running our whole-house humidifier along with the air conditioning during the summer. Is this a good or bad idea? I thought air conditioning took all the humidity out of the air.

I wouldn't come right out and say this is a vacuous idea, but I don't think it is a very good plan.

A humidifier obviously puts moisture in the air. An air conditioner cools the air by taking most of the moisture out of it.

So you're kind of working at cross-purposes, here, don't you think? You're pitting the humidifier against the AC and just burning up electricity in the meantime.

Granted, the air is a tad dry this time of year—single-digit humidity readings are common just now. It kind of dries you up.

Here's my vacuous thought on the matter: If you find the dry air uncomfortable, you should get an evaporative cooler—a swamp cooler.

Until the monsoon gets here, an evaporative cooler will cool the air without sucking out all the humidity. After the monsoon gets here, the last thing you're going to want is more humid air. Plus, a swamp cooler is a lot cheaper to run than an air conditioner.

Let me adjust my glove before I step into question box

July 9, 2010

So today we shall lead off with a question I have for you people instead of the other way around.

How many times during a single at bat should the batter be allowed to step out of the box and adjust the Velcro straps on his batting glove before the umpire is permitted to give him a dope slap with a rubber chicken?

I say one, but, as always, I am open to your thoughts on this matter.

Congress is the combination of both the Senate and House of Representatives. So why are House members referred to as congressmen while Senate members, even though they are part of Congress, are only referred to as senators?

That's a good question, and I'm not sure I can answer it very well.

The only explanation I could come up with is that the Senate is considered to be a more exclusive institution and its members are thought to be a higher life form than mere congressmen/women.

So they are called senators as a mark of respect.

That's the best I could come up with. What do you think?

I have noticed how confused people are when they get to a stoplight, and there is no "No turn on red" sign but there is a sign that reads "Wait for green." Is it legal to turn on red? Do you have to wait for green in order to make a legal right turn? I take the assumption I can turn right on red unless there is a specific sign telling me I can't.

I'm trying to decide if this is one of those phony questions that make me look like the dummy I am questions. However, knowing you people as I do, I am going to reply anyway.

What part of "Wait for green" don't you understand? If the sign says you have to wait for the green arrow, it means you can't turn on red.

Dust storm could bring scorpion in on the wind

July 13, 2010

The day after last week's big storm, we found a small scorpion in our garage. We live in central Phoenix and have never seen a scorpion before. Is it possible that it was blown in by the wind?

Gee, I don't know. Remember those flying monkeys from "Wizard of Oz"? I bet they might get blown into your garage in a big wind.

How creepy would that be? They always gave me the heebie-jeebies.

As for scorpions, they have fairly sticky legs that help, at least some varieties, crawl up trees and stuff and keep them from being blown away in a gale.

On the other hand, it was a pretty strong storm, wasn't it? I suppose a really strong wind might have scooped up a small scorpion and set it down in or near your garage.

Or maybe the scorpion, unbeknownst to you, was already there and just crept into your garage to seek shelter.

Either way, I'd take a small scorpion over those flying monkeys any day.

At least with a scorpion you can sweep it into a dustpan and throw it over the fence into your neighbor's yard, provided your neighbor isn't around at the moment.

We often have quail with fledglings in our yard. Recently, we have seen two mature males with seven fledglings but no mature female. What gives?

Did you know that the word "quail" comes from Middle Dutch by way of an Old French word meaning "quack"? I guess old French people thought that a quail's call sounded like a duck's.

Those wacky old French people.

Anyway, quail, both male and female, are pretty good parents. If some misfortune should befall the female, it is not unusual for the male to take over the parenting duties.

Do bunnies have a death wish?

July 15, 2010

I live in an area where there are a lot of cottontail rabbits that appear to have a death wish. They run across the path of my car instead of away from it, sometimes from a considerable distance away from the road. Why do these dumb bunnies have such a seemingly counter-productive instinct? I have tried to imagine what in nature would be analogous to an approaching automobile and why cutting across in front of it would be a smart move. With child-like trust, I turn to you.

Child-like trust. That's kind of sweet, isn't it? It implies that this gentle soul is counting on me to do some serious research about this and come up with an actual, factual answer.

Sucker.

OK, I take that back. It was unnecessarily snarky, wasn't it?

Part of the answer may be that because of the way their eyes are situated in their heads, rabbits don't have especially good three-dimensional vision. And that means the farther away something is, the less it appears to be moving.

But I think the main thing is panic.

Creatures such as rabbits or raccoons or chupacabras might become so disoriented by your vehicle hurtling toward them that they lose their senses and make a run for safety, which might take them right in front of you. OK, maybe not chupacabras—"goat suckers"—since there are no such things. This panic thing might be especially true at night when they are further disoriented by your headlights.

It's sort of like our young news clerks when they see one of the masters approaching to shake them down for their lunch money. They just empty their pockets and run willy-nilly, sometimes right into the path of danger.

Facing a skunk, it's best just to walk away

July 18, 2010

Recently, when my husband and I were returning from an evening walk, we saw a skunk in our front yard that we would have to pass to get into the house. We stopped as soon as we saw it, not knowing what to do. Luckily, it soon ran off in the opposite direction. Can you tell us what to do in such a situation if the skunk doesn't leave? Just wait it out? Make loud noises to frighten it away? It's not just the danger of the spray but the fact that it could be rabid.

This one is from a lady in Prescott, but that doesn't mean that if you live here in the Valley you're off the hook, skunk-wise.

Did you know we have four varieties of skunk in Arizona? Striped, spotted, hooded and hog-nosed and, to one degree or another, most of them are found around these parts.

You certainly don't want to get sprayed by a skunk, nor do you want to you have your pet get sprayed. The spray not only smells terrible, but it also is kind of oily, which means it's hard to get rid of.

As for what to do if you meet a skunk on the path, this lady and her husband pretty much did the right thing.

Skunks don't really want to put the stink on you any more than you want to receive it. Just as I feel about my masters, they would just as soon be left alone.

They are accurate with their spray from 10, maybe 20 feet, so should you happen to come across one, the best thing to do is just back away.

If you try to scare it off by waving your arms or shouting or trying to shoo it away, you're probably only going to annoy it and make it feel threatened.

Then it will stamp its little skunk feet, maybe growl in a skunk sort of way and, if it feels seriously threatened, raise its skunk butt and let you have it.

So just walk away slow.

Animals sense storms through change in air pressure

July 19, 2010

How does our cat know there is a storm coming? She is terrified of rainstorms, and will hide under the bed if she hears raindrops on the roof. We live near Cactus Road and Tatum Boulevard, and if there is a storm as close as Fountain Hills or Carefree, her eyes get big as saucers. Is there something electrical that she can sense, or a change in air pressure or what?

It's air pressure.

Dogs and cats and other critters, including some people, are sensitive to the changes in air pressure that a storm brings.

It seems to affect different animals in different ways. For instance, my dog Dumb could care less if there is a storm in the area, even if it's right over the house. On the other hand, my other dog, Dumber, goes nuts when it's stormy and has to be tranquilized. She once jumped through a closed window during a storm.

Many people with old scars or creaky joints or whatever can tell when the weather is changing by the aches and pains that the change in air pressure brings them.

Some time ago, I saw a map showing the distance between streets when hiking the canal. Can you tell me where this information might be available?

I found two sites that you may find helpful.

The Salt River Project has a canals-distances calculator at srpnet. com/water/canals/distances.aspx. Or you can go to scottsdalerun-ningco.com.

What is the plural of computer mouse—mouses or mice?

The Compact Oxford English Dictionary and other sources I checked say either mouses or mice is OK.

The plural "mouses" treats mouse as a "headless noun," although I have no idea what that means.

Ramps bring runaway trucks to a halt... most of the time

July 29, 2010

As I travel through the mountainous areas of the state, I've noticed runaway truck ramps. When's the last time one of these ramps was used? I figured if anyone would know, it would be you.

Why would I know something like that?

It is true that I have learned a lot of more or less interesting stuff answering questions from you people, but after a week or so almost all of it goes to the "empty recycle bin" department in my brain.

So on the odd chance I actually knew the answer to your question I would have forgotten it by now, along with where I put the owner's manual for my cell phone.

Anyway, those runaway truck ramps are pretty cool, aren't they? I always wanted to try one, even though I didn't have a truck nor was my vehicle by any means running away or even capable of doing so, but my daughters and their mother always dissuaded me from this.

As a rule these ramps are made up of gravel—or, in some states, sand—that cushions the energy of a runaway big rig and brings it to a stop.

However, I did read one account of a runaway lumber truck in the Lake Tahoe area that shot up and over a ramp and crashed into an expensive house below. It sounds like a horrible thing, but you have to admit it would have been something to see.

Anyway, I put this matter to Doug Ninztel, an esteemed spokesman for the Arizona Department of Transportation, and he said he didn't have all the figures, but the number of trucks using those ramps seems to average around one a month, give or take.

I doubt if that includes dumb guys in dumpy family sedans who might think it would be cool to give one a shot.

Can you give a mosquito a buzz?

August 9, 2010

Suppose there is a party of the patio and everybody has a few drinks. If a mosquito bites someone with a high blood alcohol level, will it get a buzz—pun intended?

So, in other words you had a patio party and didn't invite me, huh? Story of my life. Well, fine. It's too hot for a patio party anyway.

First of all, yes, mosquitoes are more attracted to people who had a few toots. Researchers in Burkino Faso—that's in West Africa—exposed a group of men to a bunch of mosquitoes. At first they found the mosquitoes showed no preference between ordinary human odors and fresh air. However, after the men each drank a liter of low-alcohol beer, the mosquitoes picked their aromas over fresh air by a margin of 2-to-1.

Do you know what an inebriometer is? It's a device that scientists use to test a bug's sensitivity to alcohol by blowing puffs of ethanol at them. Some of them can withstand concentrations of up to 60 percent.

It seems that mosquitoes can tolerate the stuff better than some other insects, perhaps because they also feed on rotten fruit or plants which would contain alcohol of up to 1 percent. That would help build up their tolerance.

According to something I read from Coby Schal, an entomologist at North Carolina State University, a mosquito taking a blood meal from a person who had had 10 drinks would be getting the equivalent of one beer watered down 25-fold.

Also, mosquitoes have a sort of holding bag for any fluids other than blood. Enzymes in that bag break down those fluids before they hit the nervous system.

So what it comes down to is that you could get a mosquito drunk but to do so you'd have to drink enough to kill you.

No foolin' around: You don't want to be a 'grass widow'

August 19, 2010

Today's question is sort of a condensed version of a longer inquiry from some lady who wants to know:

What is a "grass widow," and where did that phrase come from?

This is from a very nice person—at least she sounded nice in her message—who is in a support group for widows, and this apparently came up during one of their sessions.

The origins of "grass widow" seem to be the subject of some debate among people who care to debate about such matters.

One idea is that the term refers to an unmarried woman who has been—kids,: ask Mommy or Daddy about this part—fooling around in a pasture or some other expanse of grass with a partner who afterwards lost interest in their relationship.

Now, thanks to my career in agribusiness in my younger days, I'm not sure I would want to fool around in a pasture—or any other spot involving Holsteins or other such beasts—with any co-fool-arounder, but there you have it.

Another explanation, and probably the most likely, is that the phrase refers to a woman whose husband has divorced or deserted her, as in a jerk who has "put her out to pasture."

I didn't know about that before, because for some reason I'd always thought the phrase meant a woman neglected by a husband who preferred playing golf to the company of his wife. But then, what do I know?

Americans are referred to by the British as Yankees. What is the origin of this?

Nobody seems to know for sure, but it probably is some mangling of "John Cheese,"—think "Y" for "J"—a derogatory term used by Dutch settlers in the New World to refer to their neighboring British colonists in Connecticut.

Do I sound like Charlton Heston or George Clooney?

August 31, 2010

Why does my voice sound different when I hear it on a recording than it does when I hear it in my head?

Good question. I know just what you mean.

When I speak, I hear my rich, resonant and manly tones and I am reminded of Charleton Heston or George Clooney and always wonder why more women don't swoon or go all kissy-face when they hear such a voice.

But when I hear my recorded voice, I sound all tinny and whiney.

Sometimes I think I should take a vow of silence and just communicate, if needed, by means of notes.

Actually, I've been meaning to see, just out of curiosity, what it would be like to go a whole day without speaking. When it's just you and the dogs and you don't have anything in particular to do that day, it could be done.

But I keep forgetting and call the dogs to come in or go out, which they would do anyway, or ask them if they'd like a treat— duh. And I keep discussing you people and your questions and comments with them. I don't know why. They really don't seem all that interested.

But I digress.

When you hear a recording of yourself, you hear the way your sound waves travel through the air to the microphone.

However, when you speak, your brain hears something else. That rascal hears the sound of your voice as it reverberates through your sinus cavities and the bones in your head and so on and so forth and all that turns out a different kind of sound, the kind that should make the opposite sex go all kissy-face and sort of weak at the knees.

Or maybe the same sex.

Such matters t'aint no business of mine.

A new labor policy

September 13, 2010

You will be pleased to know—or maybe just interested or maybe even repulsed—that I have come up with a new idea about working. I hope it is one you can benefit from.

This came upon me because I was thinking about an old friend who now lives in Seattle or Saskatchewan or someplace like that that starts with an S.

Anyway, I was thinking about the last time I called her and her telling me she was putting in 50 to 60 hours at her new job.

So, I was thinking about this and ruminating on it when my new idea about working came to me.

Here it is: The more time you spend at work or thinking about work, the more likely you are to screw up or think up an especially bad idea.

And you might compound that error by suggesting that idea to your masters—and having no ideas themselves, there is the danger they might put it to use.

I've been thinking on this and doing the math, and I have concluded that if you are supposed to work a 40-hour week —assuming you have a 40-hour-a-week job—and goof off so much that you really are working only 20 hours, you would cut in half your chances of doing something wrong that might put your job in jeopardy.

And speaking of jeopardy, watching "Jeopardy" is an excellent way to goof off.

So, for your own benefit and for the best interests of your employer, I think you should not work anymore than necessary in order to hold down the risk of mistakes or coming up with and executing an especially bad idea.

And should your boss question you about this policy that I inspired in you, just show him or her a clipping of this column and you'll be pretty much assured of, shall we say, a new position in life.

You can't get pregnant from touching a restaurant statue

September 23, 2010

A friend of mine has been trying to get pregnant with no success. We heard about a restaurant in Mesa that has a fertility statue. When a woman touches it, she gets pregnant. We haven't been able to find any information on said restaurant. Have you heard about it?

No, I haven't heard of it and although I did make a cursory search, I am not inclined to pursue this matter.

Look, if you really are your friend's friend, I think you need to sit down with her and explain that she can't get pregnant by touching a statue in a restaurant.

Perhaps she doesn't know this, but, with a few variations, the only way she is going to get pregnant is by…umm…the standard method.

If you are uncomfortable with this, perhaps you could find a helpful illustrated book for her at your local library. Libraries are useful that way.

Do you remember those X-ray machines they used to use to check if the shoes you bought were the right size? You could see your feet in the shoes and watch your toes wiggle. Whatever happened to them? I bet you are too young to remember them.

Whether I am too young to remember such devices isn't any of your business. Maybe I am and maybe I'm not.

X-ray fluoroscope machines—sometimes called *pedoscopes*—were very popular in shoe stores from roughly 1930 to 1960. They gave you an X-ray of how your shoes fit and how your weight was distributed on your feet and so on.

Their popularity waned in the '60s when people began to realize that those machines were giving users a dose of radiation to their tootsies that was way, way above the daily allowance allowed today for workers in nuclear power plants.

How to hang a horseshoe properly and catch good luck

September 24, 2010

We have a controversy about the proper way to nail a horse shoe over a door. Legs up or legs pointed down?

Got some time on your hands, huh?

I shouldn't be snarky about this. It actually turned out to be interesting, or at least semi-interesting.

There are two schools of thought on this matter. Some people say you should hang the horseshoe with the ends—the heels—pointing up so the good luck it brings won't drain out.

Others say the heels should be pointing down so the good luck falls on anybody passing through the doorway.

The interesting bit is the origin of the horseshoe superstition.

One story has it that the devil went to a blacksmith to get his hooves shod. So the smith shaped the horseshoes and nailed them—red hot—into Satan's hooves.

The devil went on his way, but soon the hot horseshoes and nails caused him such agony that he tore them off and never went near a horseshoe again.

Another idea is that horseshoes are lucky because they are made by blacksmiths, who were considered to be lucky in the old days. That was because they worked with fire—one of the basic elements—and iron, which was believed to possess magic because it was stronger than other metals and could survive a fire.

Blacksmiths were so lucky, the ancients believed, that they could heal the sick.

And horseshoes were nailed on with seven nails, and seven was a lucky number in many ancient cultures.

So hang your horseshoe any old way you want, and I hope it brings you good luck.

It won't, of course, but it's a nice thought.

Sniffing all around for leaping coyotes and singing dogs

September 25, 2010

Have you ever heard of New Guinea singing dogs?

Neither had I until I happened across some stuff about them while researching another question.

A New Guinea singing dog is a very rare breed of canine probably brought to New Guinea thousands of years ago by ancient voyagers. They are sort of related to the Australian dingo.

They get their name from their melodious—some say eerie—style of howling. You can hear it at www.metacafe.com, but you're going to have to fish around in there a bit to get at it. Or maybe I should say sniff around.

It seems that if you look hard enough, you can find a New Guinea singing dog breeder in this country, and while I'm sure they're perfectly fine animals, I'm not sure I would want a dog that is only a few steps removed from being a wolf hanging around.

I have enough problems dealing with Dumb and Dumber. I worry sometimes that one of these days they will forget to inhale and exhale. Of course, I've had the same worries about some of my masters.

Anyway, the question I was researching when I came across New Guinea singing dogs was this: Can a coyote scale a 6-foot-high wrought iron fence?

Now I know a coyote can jump a high block fence, and I am tempted to say the beast couldn't get enough of a foothold on a wrought iron fence to pull itself over and get at little Puff or Spot.

However, after many years of answering your questions about coyotes—and being corrected by you people for some of those answers—I am not prepared to say "never" about coyotes. Maybe they're not able to fly or vote or anything like that, but they are crafty rascals.

On 'lobotomized goldfish' and hair-garnished falafel

October 9, 2010

I think maybe it's time to get out my autumn bathrobe, the one with the leaping deer on it.

You know what? I've lived here for a long time and, I don't know about you, but I think it is weird to feel cold when the morning temperatures are in the 70s.

Now, one last word about the question the other day from the guy who thought his 60-year-old wife is too old to be wearing thong underwear.

I wondered if it was a made-up question and opined that he should mind his own business.

Anyway, I just got a nice letter from the wife in question and she said it was a genuine question and she agreed with my answer. She also assured me she weighs 110 and doesn't look gross in her thong.

And she said she loves her husband and he is smart about many things, but sometimes, he can be "as dumb as a lobotomized goldfish." That puts that matter to rest. Let's move on.

Recently, I was enjoying lunch in one of my favorite restaurants when I found a hair in my falafel. I inconspicuously plucked it out and kept eating. Who knows? It could have been one of mine. What harm does a hair pose if it's someone else's? I didn't feel very well that night, and I'm just wondering what I might have exposed myself to.

Do you know what chaetophobia is? It's a fear of hair.

But that's not what you asked about, is it?

Any foreign body in your food could make you sick.

Why do you think food-service workers are required to wear hair nets?

I don't necessarily know that a single hair could make you too sick. I mean, it's not like you found crushed glass in your meal. Still, I think you should have sent your falafel back.

Does rainwater make lawns look nicer than city water?

October 21, 2010

I'm not sure if this is your area, but how can I find the crossword puzzle?

Huh?

Let's do this one instead.

My lawn seems to look better after a good rain. Is there something in rainwater that is different than using city water?

Weren't those rains a treat? Not to mention the cooler weather.

I woke up in the middle of the night the other night and it took me a second or to realize what was wrong: I was cold. I guess I'd forgotten what it was like.

As for your rainwater and your lawn: It does seem that if rain water isn't too spoiled by air pollution it is better for the plants than city water out of the hose.

It seems to contain lots of nitrogen. I also read that it has a lot of hydrogen peroxide, but I don't know if that's true, and I don't know what your plants would want with hydrogen peroxide.

City water, by necessity, has a small amount of chlorine or other chemicals in it to keep it clean. You wouldn't go around spraying your plants with bleach, would you?

One other thing: If you ware watering your lawn with sprinklers, rain supplies a little bit more even coverage, no matter how well your sprinklers are aimed.

We have dragonflies hooked up tail-to-nose flying low over our driveway. I assume they are mating. We have painted our driveway green, and it's the only green driveway in the area. And we are the only ones who have these dragonflies. Is it the color green that attracts them? What else could it be?

As far as I can tell, dragonflies are not picky about colors.

What they really like is water.

Do you or some nearby neighbor have a pond where the dragonflies might lay their eggs or find mosquitoes to eat?

Sussing out the sweatshirt and pigmentation situations

October 25, 2010

Now that the weather has cooled off, I have unpacked my sweatshirt collection for the season.

There are ratty sweatshirts for working in the yard or around the house. There are my less ratty sweatshirts for office work and my hardly-ratty-at-all sweatshirts for dining out or church.

I could go into greater detail, but we have work to do.

The other day on the radio I heard a reporter say so-and-so was "sussing" something out. It seemed to mean that person hunting for something. Where did this new word come from?

According to the "Oxford English Dictionary," it dates back to the 1930s. Its meaning seems to have evolved over the years.

In the 1960s, "suss" was widely used in Britain as a verb to mean "to suspect" and as a noun to mean "suspicion" or a "suspect," as in, "They arrested the guy on suss."

Over time its definition has expanded to include "knowledge" or "to search for information." "We had to suss out this guy's history. Then we had the suss on him."

Why is it that many, if not most, of the wild plants and flowers in Arizona have yellow blooms? The predominant color when the desert is in bloom seems to be yellow.

Gee, I don't know. I am reluctant to make a blanket statement on this. Blanket statements almost always get me in trouble.

Plants that rely on pollinators such as birds or bees or bats need bright colors to attract them.

And it is true that there does seem to be an awful lot of yellow out there, but there are also plenty of blues and reds and oranges. Prickly pears, for example, come in yellow, red or orange.

And it would be pretty boring if everything were yellow, don't you think?

Does your fish look zoned out? He's probably asleep

November 10, 2010

From what desert plant, cactus or tree do devil's horns come?

They don't come from any plant. They are a plant in and of themselves.

Devil's horns are a succulent, a variety of crassula. They have green leaves that turn red if they are cold or underfed.

When it rains the tips of the "horns" turn red. Devil's horn is also the name for a group of muscles under your belly button that involves your hip inductors. They get that name because they are shaped like an inverted pyramid. If you're in skinny and in really good shape, they stand out very well.

My husband and I have been going fishing at Lake Pleasant at night. We've caught a few. My question is, do fish ever sleep?

Everything sleeps in one way or another. OK, not rocks or stuff like that, but everything else.

Fish don't sleep like you do, but they do go into a sort of trance-like state in which their metabolism slows down and they are not very active.

If you looked at your goldfish late at night you might see it just sort of hanging in the water making only slight motions with its fins to maintain its equilibrium.

Some fish rest on the bottom to catch a few fish zzzzzzs. Others, such as sharks, "sleep" while in motion.

This is interesting: parrotfish wrap themselves in a kind of mucus cocoon when they rest.

If the president and vice president both die or are incapacitated the speaker of the House becomes president. If that were to happen before the next Congress is seated and Nancy Pelosi became president, would she have to step down in January when the new speaker was elected?

No, she would serve until the next presidential election.

What's eating the flowers? Perhaps not what you think

November 18, 2010

My husband and I moved to Arizona from Indiana two years ago. In Indiana, I always planted flowers and had no problem. Two weeks ago, I planted pansies. Within the first week, the birds—doves or quail— had eaten all the blossoms. The next week, they ate the entire plant. Now I have a lovely clay bowl of dirt. Is there another plant I can plant that birds don't eat?

First of all, are you sure it's the birds that are to blame? I'm not saying they might not be, but it could be the birds are hopping around in your pots looking for grubs or bugs while some other culprit—maybe a rabbit—is chewing up the plants.

Next, I'm told birds don't like the iris and daffodils, but I don't know if that's really true.

You might try coiling a rubber snake around your flowers, adjusting its position every now and then. Or you might try hanging wind chimes or CDs or strips of foil near your flowers.

To tell you the truth, your best bet would be to call the gardening experts at the Maricopa County Extension Service at 602-827-8200. They, unlike me, actually know what they're talking about.

My father's mother came to the United States from Spain in the late 1800's. She then married a Mexican from Texas. Every generation since then has married a Mexican. To this day, my mother insists that we are Spanish and not Mexican. So my question is, what are we—Spanish or Mexican? We are not Latino or Hispanics as those are a group of people, not a nationality.

Gee, I don't know.

I would say you arc Americans with a Mexican heritage. On the other hand, if your mother wants to insist you're Spanish and it makes her happy, what's the harm in that?

Your vermillion border makes you human

December 18, 2010

My 19-year-old daughter, who is an artist, asked me why our lips are of a different tint than the rest of the face. I told her it would look weird if they weren't, but she wants more details.

You must not be much of a father if you gave her a perfectly good answer and she still insists on more details. I mean, where's the trust? Where's a daughter's unfailing belief in her father's infallibility?

OK, tell her this: The skin on your lips is very thin, compared to the skin on the rest of your face. That means the little blood-delivering capillaries are a lot closer to the surface and makes your lips kind of pinkish or rosy.

When you are really cold, your lips turn blue because those little capillaries withdraw from the surface to conserve the heat at your body's core.

And your lips don't have a lot of melanocytes, the cells that produce melanin pigments.

Why is the skin on your lips so thin?

I don't know for sure, but I'm guessing that thin-skinned, sensitive lips helped our knuckle-dragging ancestors to decide if it was a good idea or not to eat stuff they might have picked up at random. Or maybe there are some other reasons involved.

Here's something interesting: There is a sort of an outline or border around your lips called the vermillion border. It is sort of a transition from the color of the skin on the rest of your face to the color of your lips. Only humans have this.

Why? Nobody knows.

More stuff: Ladies, if you rub a bit of salt or cayenne pepper on your lips, it will give them that sort of bee-stung reddish look, which gives men the idea, right or wrong, that you would not be averse to their advances.

Space bocks them off, but the sun does makes sounds

January 27, 2011

Why can't we hear the sun?

You can.

Go to www.shef.ac.uk/mediacentre/2010/1662.

It's a short recording made by Robertus von Fay-Siebenburgen, head of the solar-physics team at the University of Sheffield in the United Kingdom.

Robertus von Fay-Siebenburgen. That's a pretty impressive name, don't you think?

He did this by using a solar orbiter to measure the magnetic vibrations of the sun's corona and turned them into sounds and enhanced them so you can hear them.

I have read various descriptions of the sound, including a volcano, a kettle drum and a cross between the last chord of the Beatles' "In My Life," and a whale's song.

The sound had to be enhanced because it is too low to be heard by the human ear.

The core of the sun is more or less a huge nuclear-fission engine where hydrogen is transformed into helium at temperatures of about 27 million degrees Fahrenheit.

This sets of waves bounce around inside the sun before rising to the surface, causing the surface to oscillate. Thus the sounds the University of Sheffield team was able to record.

And, of course, we can't hear the sun because sound doesn't travel through space.

Sometimes, my credit card doesn't work when I swipe it but if I put it in a plastic bag and swipe it it works. Why?

The magtnetic strip on your card card contains a bunch of little magnetic dots that are translated by the reader.

If some of those dots get damaged by wear and tear or dirt, the bag covers up the bad dots and, assuming the card isn't too badly damaged, allows enough good data to get through.

Hiccup relief: another real-life application for math

February 15, 2011

I have at hand a note from one of you people who wants you to know that if someone else has the hiccups, it is possible to stop them by asking them to multiply numbers.

I have no idea if this is so because I have not been around anyone with the hiccups for some time. But you people never fail to scintillate.

Is it possible to bake a square pie?

Well, I don't see why not. Some people might call it a strudel or maybe a cobbler. Myself, I am kind of a traditionalist and prefer my pies in wedge-shaped slices, but then I guess pie is pie.

You might have trouble finding square or rectangular store-bought crusts and might have to make your own, but I am sure you can figure it out. And if you Google "square pie recipes," you will find some recipes that I am far too lazy to reproduce here.

When you take a pain-relief pill, how does the pill know how to go to the part of your body that is in pain?

This may come as a surprise to some of you, but pills are not sentient beings. You cannot tell them which part hurts.

Let's take aspirin for an example.

When part of you hurts, the cells involved produce a hard-to-spell enzyme that in turn produces an equally hard-to-spell chemical that causes inflammation and also sends a message to your brain that you're hurting.

The chemicals in aspirin glom on to those enzyme-producing cells and more or less tell them to shut up and stop making that hard-to-spell chemical so your brain doesn't get the message that something is wrong and the inflammation and swelling are reduced.

Four Peaks amethyst has a rich history, literally

February 20, 2011

Is it true that some amethyst from Four Peaks ended up in the Spanish crown jewels?

I think so. I found a couple of different references to this, but none of them was were very specific, so I don't know for sure.

One site said Four Peaks amethyst decorated the crowns of Spanish kings and those of four other European countries after it was sent back by Spanish explorers who first discovered the lode in the 18th century.

Much of the best amethyst is cut from the earth by hand at a privately- held mine. It is rated "Siberian" in grade—that's very, very good—and is prized for its reddish-purple hue, a color of royalty and nobility.

The mine is supplied by helicopter. It can be reached by four-wheel drive and an arduous hike, but if you did get there, they wouldn't let you in.

Amethyst can be found in other Four Peaks rocks, but it generally isn't of the same high quality.

The name "amethyst" comes from a Greek word meaning "not drunken."' That could be from the belief that amethyst diminished the effects of alcohol or from the stones' deep purple, wine-like color.

Why are alcoholic beverages sometimes referred to as "spirits"?

I'm a little fuzzy on this one, but then that is not an unusual state of affairs for me, as some of you might have noticed.

"Spirits" usually refers to the hard stuff—gin or rum or vodka, among others.

It seems to be a very old word. It might go back to the language of Arabic scientists who—rightly—noted alcohol had spirit-altering properties.

In Europe, alchemists in the early 17th century considered spirits to be a "volatile substance." It took on its meaning of alcoholic drinks around 1770 or so.

Dogs—not girlfriends—love ear scratches, belly rubs

March 16, 2011

I have a confession to make, something I've been holding in myself for a long time.

Please don't hate me for this, but I don't think Dennis the Menace is funny. If I were Mr. Wilson, I'd get a restraining order against the little jerk.

There, I said it. I feel better already, although I do find today's question a tad disturbing.

Why does my dog like it so much when I scratch behind his ears? I scratched my girlfriend behind her ears and got no reaction at all.

You scratched your girlfriend behind her ears? Like you would do to your dog? Are you out of your mind?

You got no reaction at all? You're lucky she didn't tear off your arm and beat you to death with it.

Guys, guys, guys: I get accused sometimes of cherry-picking the men/women questions in favor of the women, but go back to the top and read this one again. And again, I ask the guy who sent this in: Are you out of your mind?

Anyway, a dog's ears are very sensitive and have a lot of nerves, some of which are also hooked up to some internal organ.

So when you gently scratch its ears or the area behind the ears, it makes the dog feel good all over.

It might also may have something to do with being favored by the alpha male or female of the pack—you.

Many dogs also like belly rubs. Rolling over to expose their vulnerable bellies is a sign of submission, but also a sign of trust. Your dog knows you love it and won't disembowel it.

This is interesting—pet prairie dogs like to have their bellies rubbed, too. Don't ask me why anyone would keep a prairie dog as a pet. I don't know.

For that matter, pretty much any vertebrate—including us—likes to have its back or some other spot rubbed.

To scorpion, getting flushed might be like a water ride

March 21, 2011

I hate killing bugs. It's bad karma. So, when I see a scorpion in the house, I use a pair of kitchen tongs to pick it up and I flush it down the toilet. I feel that it has a 50/50 chance of surviving the flush. Do you know if they can survive being flushed down a toilet?

First of all, scorpions aren't bugs. They are arthropods but in a different group than insects. They have eight legs and are more closely related to spiders and horseshoe crabs than they are to insects. That makes them even more creepy, if you ask me.

Next, as near as I can tell, the effects of flushing on scorpions is pretty much a Ph.D. dissertation waiting to happen. I couldn't find anything on the topic one way or another.

However, if I had to make a bet I'd bet they could survive a flush. Scorpions are tough. They are hard to kill. They can survive temperatures as low as minus-13 degrees. They can go for as long as a year without eating, and some can live under water for two days or more. So, I'm thinking a scorpion would consider a flush down the toilet as some kind of water-park ride. But, as I said, I don't know that for sure.

I am from Iowa, and I am fascinated by the saguaro cactus. Why is it that the base of the cactus does not increase in circumference relative to the upper portion as the cactus grows? Saguaros look top-heavy.

I'm not sure I understand your question. A saguaro's circumference grows along with the rest of the plant. Do you mean a cactus should be as big around as it is tall? That would be silly.

Saguaros are a bit top-heavy, I suppose, but they are fairly sturdy. And they are sort of flexible. During the monsoon, their girth can expand by as much as 20 percent as they take in water.

Rattlesnakes can come after you in your bass boat

April 23, 2011

I have at hand a long question—too long to run here in its entirety—from a guy who says a swimming rattlesnake repeatedly tried to get into his boat while he and a pal were fishing at Lake Pleasant. He wants to know how long a rattler can live in the water.

Rattlesnakes don't spend a lot of time in the water, but they will take to it readily to get to food or a mate or a refuge.

They are pretty good swimmers and they can strike while in the water but not very far because they can't coil to get a base.

This guy's snake, he said, was in the water for about two hours, so I guess he kind of answered his own question.

But this is interesting: I read an account of an Eastern diamondback that was found in the Atlantic Ocean 30 miles from land. I wonder if that's true. And I wonder what that snake thought it was doing.

I also found a video of a rattlesnake trying to get into a bass boat. The address for it is pretty long and confusing, but you can find it if you Google "bassfan tv rattlesnake."

I doubt if the rattlesnake in question here was actually trying to attack the guys at Lake Pleasant. Why would it? I don't think rattlers strike just for the heck of it.

I bet it was just tired and wanted to crawl into the boat to take a rest.

Or maybe one of them had a rat in his lunch box.

Blue jays and cardinals don't hatch purple martins

April 25, 2010

My wife believes that purple martins are a result of blue jays and cardinals mating. I don't think so, but she doesn't believe me. Please settle this.

If your wife really believes this, she is a chowderhead. If you just made this question up, which I suspect you did, you are a jerk.

For one thing, we don't really have blue jays in Arizona. We had pinyon jays and Steller's jays, but not the blue jays you used to see back East.

We do, however, have purple martins. I didn't know that before, and I don't believe I've ever seen one. They seem to especially like the holes woodpeckers drill out of saguaros.

I've noticed military flyovers at outdoor events, apparently no matter how insignificant the event may be. I'm sure jet fuel costs more than $4 a gallon, and I'm curious about how this is funded. I'd like to think it's not taxpayers' money and the military somehow gets reimbursed. Does that imply the government has a facility where equipment and personnel can be made available e to the public for a price, so even I could arrange for a flyover when I walk the dog?

Yes, the jets from various arms of our military do flyovers, but I wouldn't hold my breath on that walking-the-dog thing. Besides, I'm thinking it would probably scare the bejabbers out of your dog.

As near as I can tell, these flyovers are considered to be training exercises for the pilots and recruiting tools for whichever particular service is involved.

I'm all for training pilots to fly low over ballparks or football fields or whatever. You never know when that might come in handy.

However, I can't see why anybody would be inspired to sign up just from seeing some planes fly over, but there you have it.

Be careful when hunting Arizona mushrooms

May 10, 2011

I am getting the-bird-that-sings-all-night questions again. Two alone in the last batch of e-mails.

I know for a fact this is the second time this season and the nth time over the years. Write it down this time, OK?

It is an unmated male mockingbird declaring his territory and looking for love. Why the birds think this nocturnal warbling will succeed, I'm not sure, but it must work sometimes or they wouldn't waste energy doing it.

And as long as we are on the subject, this is the time of year that you will see male mockingbirds on the top of a power pole leap a few feet into the air and then flutter down again. It's a plumage display.

In Iowa the first of May was always the time we hunted for morel mushrooms or would buy them if they were plentiful. I was talking to a friend who lives in Arizona and she said she would love to go up to northern Arizona and hunt morel mushrooms. Are there morel mushrooms in Arizona?

I'll tell you, but only if you promise to be careful. There are a lot of mushrooms out there that will make you sick or kill you, including a false morel and one with the charming name of "the western destroying angel."

That said, I am told there are morels in the Sedona area and around Flagstaff and in the areas above the Mogollon Rim that get plenty of rain. The season seems to start in May or June.

I found several websites about the mushrooms of Arizona.

This one looked good: az-mushroom-club.org. They provide mushroom-identification classes and make trips at various times of year to search for the good ones.

Just be careful, OK? I can't afford to lose any of you people.

And aren't you proud of me for not making any "fun-guy" jokes? I do have some standards, you know.

Why some coins have notches, or reeds

May 14, 2011

Why do dimes, quarters and half dollars have notches on the edge while pennies and nickels don't?

By golly, you're right. I never noticed that before.

Many years ago dimes, quarters and half dollars contained gold or silver, and people would shave a bit of the precious metals off the edges.

So the U.S. Mint started putting notches, known as reeds, on the edges to deter counterfeiting or illegal use of the coins. Pennies and nickels were not thought to be worth enough to merit shaving and thus not worth notching.

Not that you asked, but a dime has 118 reeds. A quarter has 119 and a half dollar has 150.

These days, of course, coins are composed of various alloys of copper and zinc and stuff, but they still have those reeds. I suppose they might continue to discourage counterfeiters.

Next, some housekeeping business. Pay attention now because this can get a bit confusing.

For the past few months I have been assigned to write one lengthy—to my way of thinking—story a month about some aspect of Arizona history. They run on Saturdays in the Explore Arizona section, and are part of the paper's preparations for next year's state centennial.

Last Saturday's story about Jack Swilling, the founder of Phoenix, included an editor's note that this history series is running in lieu of the regular column I had been doing with the lame-o title of Arizona 101.

As a result I heard from several of you who read that to mean the end of Valley 101 while what it was referring to was the weekly history column, which hardly anyone ever read.

So just calm down, OK? Like it or not, Valley 101 is not being dropped.

And don't write to my masters complaining about the end of Valley 101. I don't want them getting any ideas.

"Number stations" used to transmit secret messages

May 20, 2011

I wasn't going to write a column for today seeing as how it's the day the world is going to end. However, my masters allowed as how it might be my job that was going to end if I didn't produce so I decided to crank one out anyway.

To that end, I have at hand a long, long question from a lady who once came across something odd on her radio while driving across Texas.

The gist of her question is this: Trying to get away from country music, she came across an FM station where she heard an automated female voice reading nothing but a series of numbers. Naturally, she was curious about this.

Now to tell the truth, I'm not much on country music, but I'd rather listen to that than some lady just reading numbers, but that is neither here nor there.

I'm sure many of you have a better idea about this matter than I do, but what I found was that there seem to be something called "number stations" that usually broadcast on shortwave frequencies but sometimes on FM.

Now there seem to be several ideas about this, but it apparently these number stations are used by intelligence agencies in various countries to transmit encoded messages to spies. I also read that drug smugglers might use them, too. Sometimes they use strings of numbers and sometimes coded words.

Number stations may have started during World War I or maybe in World War II. There seem to be differences of opinion about this.

And they may have originally been used to transmit weather information or maybe spy stuff. This is all a little murky.

If you Google "number stations frequencies you can find a list of such things, mostly on shortwave, although why you want to listen to someone reciting a list of numbers for whatever reason beats me.

The dirt on the Grand Canyon

June 22, 2011

Do you remember a television show called "Wagon Train"?

Neither do I, but then I still have the dew of youth upon my brow.

It seems to have been about a bunch of hardy pioneers who were headed for California or Oregon or someplace like that by, not surprisingly, wagon train.

It starred, as we all know, Ward Bond, who, as we all know, played one of the police detectives in "The Maltese Falcon," which may have been the greatest movie ever made, unless it was "High Noon" or "Kung Fu Panda."

Anyway, I just got a question—I think a deliberately silly question—from somebody who wanted to know how many wagons were in the wagon train.

Sigh.

I wonder what the grown-up columnists are writing about today. The Legislature? The economy? Politics? Drug-crazed, gun-toting, godless illegal immigrants setting wildfires so they can drive Americans away so they can reclaim Arizona and California and so on for Mexico and send their children to our schools for free and take over and make the rest of us wear our underpants on our heads?

Whatever. Let's get down to business.

If the Colorado River carved out the Grand Canyon, where did all the dirt go?

Eons ago, what is now Yuma stood on the shore of the Sea of Cortez or the Gulf of California or whatever you want to call it.

Geologists tell us that way back then the gulf extended to the north well beyond where Yuma is today.

Over the centuries the rocks and dirt and silt the Colorado brought down from the Grand Canyon and the rest of its vast drainage basin settled either on what are now the banks of the river or formed an immense delta at its mouth.

How ants dispose of their dead

September 7, 2011

We sprayed hundreds of ants with Raid the other evening. When we woke up the dead ants were stacked in piles. Why do ants make little piles of their dead?

Hundreds? You killed hundreds of ants? I suppose it's none of my business, but why?

Were they in your house or outside? And did you have to spray them with chemicals? There are other ways of discouraging ants.

We will discuss that later, but first let's deal with the question at hand.

Ants are tidy creatures. And they communicate by chemical scents.

When an ant dies its scent changes because the corpse releases something called oleic acid. So the living bring out their dead to prevent a contamination that might harm the queen or the rest of the colony.

Some types of ants haul the dead all the way out of the colony and some use burial chambers.

Ants also carry waste material out of the colony and stack it in piles called middens.

Ants are not alone in this behavior. Bees, for example, will push their dead out of the hive.

Nobody tells the ants how to remove their dead. They are programmed to do so. This is known as swarm intelligence and some scientists study it with an eye toward understanding traffic jams or overcrowded phone lines.

Now, let's discuss how to keep ants out of your way without dousing them with a lot of chemicals.

Some people mix Borax and sugar with water and spray it around the foundation of their houses.

Or you could try scattering cinnamon around the spots where you see ants. Ants hate cinnamon.

I am told they also hate peppermint essential oil. I think you can get it at a health-food store.

Try wiping down your ant-prone areas with vinegar and then put some bay leaves around.

Human taxidermy and Western Seabord: True or False

September 10, 2011

Can taxidermy be practiced on humans?

When I was about 8, I wanted to be a taxidermist. Fortunately, or maybe unfortunately depending on your point of view, nothing ever came of that and I focused on being a cowboy instead.

As to your question, I guess it depends on what you mean by taxidermy.

What about the mummies of ancient Egypt? What about shrunken heads? What about those plasticized visible human displays that come to town every now and then?

But if you're talking about gutting grandpa's corpse and stuffing it with sawdust and some wires and giving it some glass eyes and then propping it up at the kitchen table, you'd better forget about it.

None of the 50 states permiit taxidermists to work on human bodies.

The human corpse is, for all intents and purposes, considered to be hazardous waste and states have laws about how it is disposed of. The only exception is preserving a body for scientific or educational purposes.

The East Coast is sometimes referred to as the Eastern Seaboard. Why isn't the West Coast referred to as the Western Seaboard? My husband said it used to be called that but they had to drop it because of union protests. Actually, I'm not married anymore.

Union protests? Huh? What union would protest something like that? Or why?

I think you're better off without that guy. He sounds like a doofus.

First of all, you do sometimes hear the West Coast called the Western Seaboard, but not often.

"Board" in this case is an archaic word for "border."

I guess by the time Europeans reached the West Coast in significant numbers the word had fallen out of usage.

Why do scorpions glow?
September 11, 2011

Since scorpions are nocturnal and I seldom see one in bright light, would surrounding my house with solar-cell landscaping lights keep them away?

Gee, I don't know. Scorpions, as you say, are nocturnal, but they will come out when it's light if they are hungry enough.

I suppose your plan might work, but don't you think it would look kind of goofy?

I think you'd be better off to put down a perimeter of diatomaceous earth. It chews up the bodies of scorpions and cockroaches and probably some other stuff as well.

You can get it at a nursery or hardware store.

Now in the course of working on this question, I came across something interesting. Or at least I thought it was interesting.

Now you know that scorpions glow under ultraviolet light, right? They glow kind of bluish.

There now seems to be some thought that scorpions may also glow under the light of a full moon.

The idea is that there could be enough UV rays in the light of a full moon to do the trick.

And scorpions are known to be less active when the moon is full. They tend to do their hunting under bushes. or some other source of shade.

Also, the thing of it is, is that nobody seems to know why they glow in the first place.

They might glow to find each other in the dark because their natural desert coloring would make it hard for them to otherwise find each other in the dark.

Or they might use the glow to illuminate or dazzle their prey.

It could be some sort of sunscreen, or they could use it to measure light levels so they know when it's dark enough to come out of their daytime hiding spots.

Nobody knows.

A cold nose and our number of counties

September 14, 2011

My husband thinks I'm weird, but every night my nose gets so cold that it hurts. By the morning, it's gone. Is there a reason for this?

I am tempted to side with your husband on this one, but obviously there is something going on here.

I wish you people wouldn't ask me medical questions. That's what doctors are for. For all I know you have Triple Acute Exploding Cold Nose Syndrome, if there is such a thing, and for your husband's sake I certainly wouldn't want your nose to explode in the middle of the night.

I suspect you might have some kind of circulation problem, but again I really think you ought to talk to your doctor about this.

(Just wondering and it's really none of my business, but when your nose is really cold do you ever snuggle up to your husband and sticck your cold honker into the nape of his neck while he's asleep? That might be entertaining.)

Why does Arizona have so few counties? As you move east, the states seem to have a lot more counties.

When we became a state in 1912 our Constitution called for 14 counties and that was fine until 1983 when La Paz County was carved out of the northern portion of Yuma County. La Paz was created because the folks living there were tired of traveling all the way to Yuma to conduct official business.

And that sort of answers your question.

Despite all our recent growth, much of Arizona is still fairly sparsely populated.

Coconino County, for instance, has a population density of about seven people per square mile, according to the 2010 census.

So it really doesn't make much sense to set up a lot of small administrative areas serving a relatively small number of people.

Arizona is bountful with bats

September 17, 2011

I would like to know if there are bats in Phoenix. And if there are, where would they be sleeping? I thought I saw a bat one morning last week, but my roommate said that it was just a bird.

Are there any bats in Arizona? You must be new to these parts.

Arizona has 28 species of bats. That's a lot. According to the state Fish and Game Department, that's more than almost any other state.

Where would they be sleeping? Pretty much any place where they can find a bump of at least 1/16 of an inch that they can hang onto. And they can get through an opening of just 3/8 of an inch.

You can find Arizona bats from the deserts to the mountains. They roost in caves, forests, attics, overhangs on porches and patios, under bridges, in culverts, you name it.

There are some good places for watching bats emerge for their night of hunting. Probably the best one is at the northwest corner of Camelback Road and 40th Street. There are hundreds, maybe thousands of bats living there in a flood-control tunnel. And there is a viewing stand.

You can read more about that site and others by Googling "phoenix bat cave. There are all sorts of good sites there.

A lot of people are creeped out by bats—and I have to admit I am a bit, too—but they're pretty interesting creatures.

As you know, our bat buddies eat terrific amounts of insects, many of which are of the type we don't want around.

Two of Arizona's 28 species don't eat insects—the lesser long-nosed bat and the Mexican long-tongued bat. They feed on the fruits and nectars of cactuses such as saguaros and organ pipes. They play an important role in pollinating such plants.

You may even find one of them at your hummingbird feeder sometime.

Is there such a thing as a lazy ant?

September 21, 2011

I have always wondered if is there such a thing as lazy ants, ones that sneak away and takes naps while everyone else is hard at work?

I was just going to throw this one away because it sounded kind of silly. But then if I threw out all the silly questions I get from you people, I wouldn't have much to do.

And like so many of the seemingly silly questions I get, this one turned out to be pretty interesting.

It turns out that there is such a thing as lazy ants.

For one thing, there is a rock group called Lazy Ants, but I never heard of them and they don't really have anything to do with the matter at hand.

There is a species of ant in found mostly in Japan and China—Polyergus samurai—whose workers hardly do anything at all.

Once a year or so these ants raid a nest of other ants and steal their larvae. They haul them back home and stow them away until they mature and then force the captives to do all of the colony's work.

I don't know exactly how they do this. I suppose they bite them or shove them around. Maybe they have little tiny ant cattle prods.

An article in the Oct. 15, 2010 issue of "Boston Review" cited a study by Stanford entomologist Deborah Gordon, who found that:

> *"Contrary to another of our beloved myths about ants told by Aesop, Homer, and the writer of Proverbs 6:6, many ants don't work very hard. In a large harvester-ant colony, about a third of the ants at any time are hanging around doing nothing. … Because colony behavior is regulated by a network of interactions, inactivity might have its uses. Idle ants may act as a buffer to dampen the interaction rate when it gets too high."*

I'm not quite sure why, but somehow I find all is kind of comforting.

Roadrunners aren't our only cuckoo

September 26, 2011

Following up your recent question and answer regarding roadrunners, roadrunners are classified in the family of cuckoos. Cuckoos are small and primarily a European species, although there are two varieties in America, according to the Petersen Guide. My question is: Are there larger cuckoos similar in size and behavior to the roadrunner in Europe?

This question, I must admit, is from a guy I know who is really, really smart and I am a bit surprised that he would ask me a question about anything, but there you have it,

He is correct in the idea that there are two types of cuckoos in America, sort of. There is the yellow-billed cuckoo, mostly in Florida. But there also are a couple of New World species on various Caribbean islands.

And there are various types of cuckoos in Europe, South Africa and Southeast Asia. Many are about the size of a robin.

Most of them eat stuff like insects and lizards, but some share our Arizona roadrunners' habit of whomping stuff on rocks to kill it before dinner.

You know, I once received a question from a guy who lived out on the desert somewhere and who thought their neighborhood roadrunner was bringing his wife gifts of dead stuff or sticks or whatever the way a courting male would do.

I advised him, as I recall, to try to be cosmopolitan about it and let his wife make her own decision.

Anyway, all these types of cuckoos are cousins in a way, although I don't recall any of my own cousins walking around with a half-digested snakes hanging out of their mouths the way roadrunners sometimes do.But then I'm not too sure about some of my cousins I haven't seen for quite a while.

Are female voices getting higher?

October 1, 2011

I"ve been seeking an answer to this question for some time. I have noticed over the past decade or so that females, in particular, are developing a higher pitch of voice. Females project a "baby/childlike," or what we used to refer to as a "ditzy blonde," annoying voice. Have any studies been performed regarding the chemicals in our food or some other cause that would change voice development?

My first thought was to toss this one, but as almost always happens, it turned out to be kind of interesting. Of course, as some of you know, I can be a bit dim—a quality that makes almost anything interesting.

There is no evidence that women's voices are getting higher. There is some thought that they may be getting lower.

A researcher named Anne Karpf compared recordings of women speaking from 1954 and recordings made in 1993. She found the 1993 voices were slightly lower. Not by much, but some.

Anyway, here's the part I found interesting: A 2009 study from UCLA found that the pitch of women's voices get higher during the point of their monthly cycle when they are most fertile.

The thinking was that men find higher voices more attractive, so women unconsciously make their voices higher to signal they are ready to make babies. (Studies have also found the tips exotic dancers get are higher/ when they are most fertile.)

However, a later study has indicated maybe the monthly change in a woman's voice doesn't really make much difference in courtship rituals.

A report earlier this year from the German Primate Center said the change to a higher pitch is too subtle for men to perceive.

What everyone wants to know: How do elk whistle?

October 5, 2011

I got a note the other day from a guy who said he didn't get the punch line in that day's "Doonesbury."

He wanted me to telephone "Doonesbury" creator Garry Trudeau and ask him to explain it and then put the explanation in a column.

I wouldn't hold my breath on that one, buddy.

Next, here's a question from a guy who wants to know if elk have vocal chords and, if so, do they use them to make that whistling noise bull elk sometimes make to attract females.

Sigh.

Yes, of course elk have vocal chords. How do you think they make all those elk sort of noises they make? Elk flatulence?

Elk do have two teeth in their upper jaws called whistlers or ivories, but they don't use them to whistle. That would be kind of silly.

There are two interesting aspects to this. First, elk are the only North American deerish animals that have any of those ivory teeth. They seem to be highly prized by people who highly prize stuff like such as that.

Next, at one time in their evolutionary history those teeth were more like tusks, like those of a walrus.

Those prehistoric elk used those tusks the way they use their magnificent antlers today—to fight with other males, to defend themselves against predators and to impress the prehistoric elk babes.

Actually, while today's elk are beautiful creatures, an elk with tusks would be kind of creepy, don't you think?

Try not to think about that while you're awake at 2 a.m., staring at the ceiling and wondering about the scariest thing that might ever happen to you.

Like skydiving or drowning or suddenly finding yourself kicking the winning the field goal for the Cardinals during a big game wearing your underwear.

Why do we dream?

October 7, 2011

What is the purpose of dreams if we can't remember them?

Isn't this great weather? I can't remember ever switching from my summer bathrobe to my autumn bathrobe this early in the season. I may even have to dig around in my closet to find my bunny slippers.

This, of course, has nothing to do with today's question. I'm just stalling for time because I don't understand the answer—or answers—very well.

The fact of the matter is that nobody knows why we dream. Researchers don't even understand the point of the REM—rapid eye movement—stage of sleep. That's when you dream.

(One idea about REM is that it helps keep your cornea supplied with oxygen while your eyes are closed.)

Sigmund Freud believed our dreams let us deal with unconscious mental turmoil.

Some folks who study such matters say dreams have no purpose at all. They say it's just your brain making random connections.

Others think your dreams are a reflection of your emotions. If, for instance, you recently experienced some kind of trauma like a near-miss car accident or escaping from a fire, you might have a dream about some other sort of scary event.

Dreams may be a way of integrating new experiences into your memory.

Or it could be an evolutionary thing. Dreams might be a kind of rehearsal for some situation in which you might find yourself. If they help you think things out, it might give some sort of evolutionary edge.

One more theory is that your memory system can become overloaded so you we dream to sort of discard the stuff we don't need.

Personally, I think parts of our brains get bored when we're asleep so they cook up dreams just to mess with us.

Here's the score

October 11, 2011

My husband says that when the Cardinals lose an away game, you say their score first so you know we're talking about the Cardinals, and then the score of their opponents. For instance, "The Cardinals lost to the Vikings 10-34." I say you always say the home team first, such as, "The Cardinals lost to the Vikings 34-10." What do you think?

You people just never run out of things to fuss about, do you? I've always wondered what the reason for that might be. Human creativity, I suppose.

Whatever.

Anyway, as far as I know, reporting the score doesn't usually have anything to do with which is the home team and which is the away team.

For instance, you wouldn't say, "The Yankees lost the seventh and deciding game of the World Series to the Chicago Cubs 0-95." No matter if the game had been played in Chicago or New York City.

Instead you would say, "The Cubs won the seventh and deciding game of the World Series 95-0. This is yet another sign of the last times."

A man with an unfaithful wife is called a cuckold. What is a woman called who is married to an unfaithful husband?

First of all, "cuckold" goes back to old French and English words referring to the habit of female cuckoos of leaving their eggs in the nests of other birds for them to raise.

As to the female equivalent: Gee, I don't know.

How about something like, "Potential ax-murderess who would cheerfully carve up that cheating son of a dog and feed his remains to the guppies?"

Well, that might work, but it seems the equivalent still draws on the cuckoo thing. It is pronounced "KUK-wean."

Don't ask me why it is pronounced like that. I don't know.

If you're going to die soon, at least find a replacement reader

October 13, 2011

If a person dies during the night and is not discovered until morning, when they are obviously dead and cold, who should be called to issue a death certificate, assuming there is no family doctor?

Why do you ask? Are you planning on dying alone at home any time soon?

I hope not. I need all of you people I can get. So if you are planning on dying anytime soon, I would appreciate it if you found a replacement, somebody who doesn't read the column now. (It shouldn't be all that hard to find someone like that.)

Anyway, when you die, you have a right to remain dead. Anything you say will be taken down and used to prove you are not dead.

And you have the right to be certified as dead by a person authorized to do so.

If you do not have such a person or cannot afford one, one will be appointed for you.

OK, this is how it works, at least in Arizona:

After they haul you off cold and dead to a funeral home, the folks there will take care of the death certificate by contacting a doctor, either by fax or in person.

And as of this year, physician assistants also are authorized to sign a death certificate.

You never see pigeons in the wild or, I should say, outside the urban areas. Is there such a thing as a "wild" pigeon? Of course, they are all wild, but it seems the mourning doves are only in the suburban areas and the pigeons are only in the cities.

First of all, you can't generalize about mourning doves in the suburbs and pigeons in the city. Next, feral pigeons go to where there is plenty of food and shelter and that means urban areas or farms.

I'm not saying you'll never see a pigeon in the wild, but I believe it would be unusual.

Mandatory HOV lane use?

October 18, 2011

I have a thing about traffic. If the police can give people a ticket for riding in the high-occupancy vehicle lane when they don't have at least two people in the car, why don't they ticket people who have two or more people that are not using the HOV lane? Seems like good sense to me. If it's going to work, people who have more than one person need to drive in that lane.

Now there's an interesting idea. I didn't say it was a very good idea. It's just interesting, as are so many of the ideas you people come up with.e

When I first read this my reaction was that more of you people should run for a seat in the Legislature where you could influence our laws.

Upon mature reflection, I decided against that. We have enough nutcases in the Legislature.

Your suggestion is, no doubt, made with the best of intentions. But I doubt if it would work.

First of all, if all the vehicles with more than one passenger were required to use the high-occupancy lane, that lane would be so crowded that it really wouldn't be of much use.

Next, don't you think our police officers and the men and women of the Highway Patrol have anything better to do than cruise the freeways looking for vehicles with more than one occupant that are not using the HOV lane?

I'd much rather that they use that time to deal with people who seem to have no concept of what their turn signals are for or what those speed-limits signs mean. Or deal with those who throw empty beer cans out the window.

Of course, I probably shouldn't talk because I don't drive on freeways if I can help it. The traffic there is either too slow or too fast or too scary and as a rule I am in no special hurry.

Forget men-vs-women game; let's talk grasshoppers

October 19, 2011

So, I was invited to speak one day last week to a group of very nice people, the Volunteer Non-Profit Service Association, the folks who put on that big used-book sale at the state fairgrounds every year to raise money for various charities.

And one of those very nice people asked me why I don't do that running score of men vs. women anymore.

It's because I was getting so many obviously made-up questions, mostly from men, that it just got to be sort of silly.

Just the day before I had given a talk to another bunch of very nice people, an organization of retired federal employees, and someone asked me if I thought women had "ganged up" on men to dominate the standings.

The obvious answer to that was no, I didn't think so because the women obviously seemed to lead the race individually without having to gang up.

Let's move on.

I live in Prescott, and our late-season grasshoppers up here look like grasshoppers until they decide to fly. Then, and only when airborne, do they resemble mourning-cloak butterflies. I've never seen them anywhere but in Arizona. What are they anyway?

Did you know there are 87 species of grasshoppers in Arizona? That strikes me as a lot.

And many of them have cool names. My favorite is the obscure-bird grasshopper.

Anyway, what you are seeing is a mourning-cloak grasshopper, also known as a Carolina grasshopper.

It is fairly common and fairly good-sized for a grasshopper. Just why it evolved to resemble a mourning-cloak butterfly while in flight, I don't know.

The butterfly, although subject to predation by a variety of creatures, is still pretty well-camouflaged, so maybe it has something to do with that.

A pure T question about flitters

November 1, 2011

I'm from Texas and sometimes I use the expression "as flat as a flitter." My son asked me what a "flitter"" is and I didn't know. Can you help?

Of course I can help, madam.

Here at the shabby but genteel headquarters of Valley 101, high above the Avenue of Broken Dreams in downtown Phoenix, we pride ourselves on being an equal opportunity column, meaning we will answer reasonable questions from anyone, even from people from Texas. I mean, you can't help it, can you?

That was probably needlessly snarky, wasn't it? Well, it was just hard to resist.

Anyway, "flat as a fritter" is a piece of Southern slang.

So is one of my favorites—"pure t." That means "really a lot" or an excellent model of." As in, "My masters are pure T cheap."

However, pure t is not the subject at hand, is it?

"Flitter" seems to be an alternative form of "fritter" and a fritter in one of its manifestations is a kind of fried batter similar to a pancake, and we have all heard the expression "flat as a pancake."

We have lived in the New River area for about 12 years. In the first couple of years we would see jackrabbits. Now it seems to be a very rare occurrence. What's going on?

Jackrabbit populations seem to be diminishing across the West, even as far east as Iowa. I didn't even know there were jackrabbits in Iowa.

It may be a sort of cyclical thing or maybe a loss of habitat.

However, the thing of it is that nobody seems to know for sure what has been happening to the jackrabbits.

How the Old Pueblo came to be the Old Pueblo

November 3, 2011

On a local television station, when the weatherman notes the temperature around the state, he frequently points out the temperature at the "Old Pueblo." It appears to be Tucson or near there. Can you enlighten us?

You're new to these parts, aint'cha stranger?

Are you one of those tenderfeet wearing big furry chaps and nickel-plated six-shooters who ties up his palomino with the silver-studded saddle and goes into the saloon and orders a sarspirilla and then beats the bejabbers out of anybody who makes fun of him?

Actually, I'm not exactly 100 percent sure what sarsparilla is, but I do know from old westerns that if you make fun of someone in big furry chaps with nickel-plated six-shooters and a palomino with a silver-studded saddle who has ordered one it's a good way to get your lights punched out, even after you hit the sarsparilla drinker over the head with a saloon chair and maybe even had thrown him over the bar.

Those sarsparilla drinkers can be nasty rascals.

Anyway, Tucson was founded in 1775 as the Presidio San Agustin de Tucson.

A presidio was a walled city and Tucson was a variation of a Native American word meaning "Place Where You Can Get Really Good Mexican Food, But You Can't Find the Restaurant Because You Get Lost Because Your Daughters Are Yapping at Each Other and Won't Give You Directions."

Or something like that.

Over time, the settlement came to be known as Pueblo de Tucson, "pueblo" being word for "village."

Afterword

Well, that's that. I hope you liked it. I hope you liked it so much you want to run out and buy some more copies for friends and loved ones. Or maybe for someone you don't like. As I believe I mentioned earlier, I need the money.

You probably can find more copies at some bookstores or at ClayThompsonBooks.com. Or you could go directly to my book publishers place and buy some there, but you'd probably end up buying some Boy Scout Christmas wreaths or stale popcorn or Girl Scout cookies or wrapping paper or something like that. Plus, their dog probably would slobber all over you.

So I'd just look in a store or go order it online, if I were you. Thanks.